The Weekend Garden

The Weekend Garden

JUDITH BERRISFORD

FABER AND FABER

LONDON   BOSTON

First published in 1978
by Faber and Faber Limited
3 Queen Square London WC1
Printed in Great Britain by
Latimer Trend & Company Ltd Plymouth
All rights reserved

© *1978 by Judith Berrisford*

British Library Cataloguing in Publication Data

Berrisford, Judith Mary
The weekend garden.
1. Gardening
I. Title
635   SB453
ISBN 0-571-11229-3
ISBN 0-571-11230-7   Pbk

Contents

Illustrations

Introduction

As gardeners whose work in journalism and lecturing often takes us abroad for quite long periods at a time, my husband and I have given a great deal of thought, and used all our ingenuity, to working out a plan whereby we can have an attractive garden to enjoy while we are at home, without it suffering too much from neglect during our absences. Basing my advice on the techniques we have successfully adopted and the lessons we have learned, I have concentrated primarily in this book on the particular needs of the owners of weekend gardens—the absent gardeners. I shall explain how to cope with drought and to defeat the weeds; which plants are the most trouble-free as regards pests and diseases; which do not need staking; which have the longest period of beauty; which will stand any necessary neglect; and which actually help in maintaining a weed-free and orderly plot.

Absent gardeners are only too well acquainted with situations with which the average garden lover does not have to cope. For them there is no possibility of nipping out to water in times of drought, no quick staking after a sudden gale, no opportunity for mowing at the optimum time, nor spraying against pests at regular intervals. Gardeners who are away for most of the week don't want to arrive home on Friday evening to find the garden a disaster area which they must spend the weekend putting to rights. Nor do they want to find that they've missed the brief flowering season of a favourite plant, or that they must spend all their short break weeding, instead of actually enjoying their gardens. They need a garden scheme which will enable them to overcome these difficulties. The answers to most of the problems common to all gardeners are to be found in a multitude of books. Here I am writing specifically for those who have to be away from their gardens for much of the time, and to this end all the available space has been devoted.

ONE

Scope and Problems

All gardeners who have to be away from their gardens for more than a few days at a stretch have the same problems—whether it is the weekend gardener who spends his or her working life in London or some other large city but enjoys retreating to the stress-free atmosphere of a country cottage at the weekend, or the average suburban dweller whose time is mostly spent at home but who wants to plan his garden so that he and his wife can get away at weekends to visit their family or take trips to the sea; anyone who is not able to devote a regular period of almost daily care to the garden must take defensive measures if it is not to suffer from their absences. Even those who spend most of their lives at home need to employ special techniques so that the garden keeps going with the minimum of deterioration when they take their annual holiday.

The obvious principle to be accepted by garden lovers whose work or pleasure takes them away often is that a small plot can more easily be kept going with irregular maintenance than a large one. 'That's all very well,' you may say, 'but we've got half-an-acre of land with our cottage and we mean to keep it all. We enjoy the privacy it confers.' Fair enough! But to retain a large piece of ground does not mean that you necessarily have to cultivate it all intensively. Decide which parts of the garden are important to you and which you can reasonably manage in the time available, and naturalize the rest.

If yours is a big rambling garden, perhaps with lawns and rose-beds near the house, and rock-gardens, flower borders and shrubs disappearing almost to infinity, why not think about preserving your treasures by moving them nearer to the house and turning the rest into wild garden, orchard or a combination of the two?

Rock-gardens as such are out of the question for the weekend or otherwise absent gardener—they need too much in the way of care. But there is nothing to prevent one growing a selection of easy alpines to give long and satisfying colour on a dry-stone wall, or as a weed-suppressing edging among the stones that bound the main flower border.

I say 'main flower border', because the easiest way of growing favourite perennials, summer bulbs, and even the strongest and sturdiest roses, is to gather them together in one large stretch. Any other borders you may decide to retain will be more trouble-free if given over to flowering and evergreen shrubs with a suitable mulch or underplanting to keep down the weeds.

Weed control is one of the most serious problems that confronts the absent gardener, along with drought which is another great difficulty, and they will both be discussed in detail in the following chapter. Luckily the two can be solved in part by the common solution you will find there.

Apart from choosing the right methods to combat these main difficulties, much of the secret of success in a weekend garden, or in any other from which the owner has frequently to be absent, lies in selecting the right plants for the right places—those which succeed naturally on the type of soil of which the garden is composed and so grow vigorously enough to keep down weed competition. If you have a wet spot, plant subjects which enjoy marshy conditions. For dry shade, choose those which occupy such positions in the wild. You will then have plants which thrive on a reasonable amount of neglect. They will tend to increase themselves and create that happy effect conferred by naturalization. They will look as if they are part of the place and not merely corseted and cosseted into survival by an ever—and often over—vigilant owner. Front gardens present a problem as they are always in the public eye. The answer here is paving—perhaps with a self-maintaining shrub surround and an island bed of shrubs for interest.

A certain informality is delightful in any garden, but it is essential in the weekend garden if its owner is to have peace of mind. By the use of correct techniques, the part of the garden nearest the house can be made to please even the tidiest-minded, in spite of frequent absences. Certain beds in our own garden have necessitated less than ten minutes' work with the trowel after a six-month period abroad. It is largely a question of careful, selective planting and mulching until the plant cover meets and becomes dense enough to keep down all weeds.

Not everyone, however, wants the whole garden to look tidy and restrained all the time. Most people enjoy a certain exuberance—a frothing bush of white *Spiraea* × *arguta* (foam of May or bridal veil); a counterpane of *Anthriscus sylvestris* (cow parsley), mingling with cowslips and columbines beneath the apple trees; the glory of a golden daffodil tide in early spring. All these can be indulged in the further confines of the garden; those parts away from the immediate surroundings of the house. They will largely look after themselves and benefit, rather than suffer, from a little masterly inattention on the part of the owner.

For the weekend gardener who spends the main part of the week in a flat, the cottage garden can be used greatly to improve his town surroundings. Bulbs in pots for winter enjoyment can be plunged in the weekend garden; after flowering they can be planted out to beautify the country plot in future seasons. Primroses, campanulas, Christmas roses and many other delights can be dug up during the weekend and potted to take back to town. The country garden can supplement the the weekday diet, too, for there are many types of fruit and vegetables which will not suffer too much, provided the gardener is there to attend to them during most weekends.

Organize the garden so that it can run itself easily with as much or as little weekend maintenance as you are willing or able to give, and from being a problem it will become the main pleasure of your country or seaside retreat, providing exercise, relaxation, cut flowers, pot plants, salads, vegetables and fruit, and generally fulfilling its purpose in enriching the quality of life, both while you are there and when you are back in town.

Twelve years ago, friends of ours bought a gardener's cottage with an acre of ground in a sheltered spot in North Wales, overlooking the sea. Business has always kept them in Liverpool during the week so that the longest period they have ever spent in the cottage was three weeks at a stretch. Some winter weekends they are unable to visit their seaside home, and during summer also, they are occasionally unable to get away. In spite of this they have year by year themselves developed the house and grounds, channelling a stream into an attractive water garden, building on a sun-porch and new kitchen, making terraces and a kitchen garden. Each year sees some new extension or plan, so that it seems the alterations will never be complete. Yet, because most of the ground is down to rough grass with fruit and flowering trees and bulbs; because they have limited the vegetable garden to an easily worked plot, scientifically mulched and planted; because the flower area is confined to two rose-beds and a wide mixed border, the place is always attractive, and our friends say that it lifts their hearts every time they leave the city and enter their own domain by the sea.

In winter *Jasminum nudiflorum* (winter jasmine) and *Chaenomeles speciosa* 'Phyllis Moore' (flowering quince), with its semi-double apricot-coloured blossoms, brighten the white-washed wall beside the porch. Lavender-coloured *Iris unguicularis* (stylosa) offers tight-furled grey buds that open to spill their delicate fragrance from the chimney-piece as the apple-logs and driftwood crackle in the grate.

In spring, daffodils are followed by cowslips, cow parsley and Queen Anne's lace (wild carrot), decorating the rough turf that runs down to the edge of the cliff. Aubrieta, yellow and buff alyssum, and white candytuft form a colourful tapestry to hang from the terrace wall. Rosemary bursts into early bloom flanking the sun-warmed stone of the steps. In the flower border, the narrowly upright *Prunus* 'Amanogawa', the maypole cherry, rises from a sea of self-sown forget-me-nots, edging the sweep of wallflowers that have been planted out to fill the vacant spaces between the rising shoots of the later-blooming perennials.

In summer lilacs bloom among the grass. Clumps of the old-fashioned cottage paeony burgeon beside the path; lime-loving clematis decorate the limestone garden wall; lupins and iris rise cleanly from the mulch that has replaced the forget-me-nots and wallflowers to act as weed-suppressing material in the border. As July turns to August there are fuchsias, revelling in the mild sea air. A variety of easy daisy flowers vie with the monkshood in the border. The deciduous *Ceanothus* 'Gloire de Versailles', hard-pruned as it was in spring, makes a cloud of blue against the cottage, tidier and longer-lasting in flower than any buddleia, and almost as efficient a butterfly-bush. In the terrace beds are roses, well cut back during the removal of the faded blooms, and sprayed against disorders, prepared for their autumn flower burst.

In autumn the berries of a trained pyracantha vie with the still-flowering fuchsias against the wall. The border is a festival of Korean chrysanthemums and late rudbeckia. The crimped, bright pink, lily-blooms of the nerines are a tribute to their sun-baked spot against the south-facing terrace wall. In the vegetable plot the last of the scarlet runners have been harvested, and the heavily laden brussels sprouts, along with late lettuce, are ready to provide good eating in the weeks ahead. The apple trees are stripped, the 'John Downie' crabs have been turned into jelly sharpened by one or two golden fruits from the ornamental quinces. Under their black polythene covering the bulbs are making strong root-growth. Later they will travel to Liverpool to brighten the sitting room from Christmas onwards.

All this has been made possible by the intelligent use of site and labour; by going along with nature rather than fighting it. Certain areas have been selected for cultivation and care—the kitchen garden to provide vegetables and salads for family needs; the flower border, rock-wall, terrace, stream and pool. The remainder is semi-wild. Fruit trees and ornamentals, placed among the grass, need only minimum care. The naturalized daffodils, cowslips, wild dog's violet and Spanish bluebells (*Endymion hispanicus*) need none. The grass itself receives two cuttings with an auto-scythe—once when the bulb foliage has died down in spring, and again in early September to allow the autumn crocus, colchicum, followed by the lavender *Crocus tomasinianus* and the striped and multi-shaded *C. chrysanthus* to bloom throughout the colder months.

In the eye of the sun, the terrace border and the beds around the house are easy to keep free of weeds by the occasional use of the hoe. Paving, grouted with cement, needs no maintenance. A thick mulch of wet peat mixed with compost prevents the emergence of weeds in the flower border. Beneath it the forget-me-not seeds (shaken out before the plants were carried to the bonfire) germinate to provide a blue mist the following spring. Wallflowers set out in autumn find the nourishment to their taste. In winter and spring the ground is carpeted with living colour until it is replaced by another organic mulch in May.

In contrast, our North Wales garden was so small that it was not practicable to leave any part wild. We liked to grow many differing plants so that there was something in flower at any time of the year whenever we happened to be at home. Another priority was that the garden should yield material for cutting throughout the year.

These criteria could have made a great deal of work, rendering it impracticable to leave the garden for long periods as we had to do; but over the years we cut out the more troublesome plants. Those that need too much staking and dead-heading were out. Bit by bit we carpeted the ground with living plant material that was at the same time attractive for use as decoration in the house. We had heathers in the front garden where the soil was shaly and thin; supplemented by dwarf azaleas and rhododendrons they made easy-care beds in the sun. Periwinkle, bugle, creeping dead-nettle, variegated ivies and hardy geraniums made attractive underplanting beneath other shrubs.

Close planting throughout the garden gave a dense branch cover that did not allow enough light through to encourage the weeds. Our main flower border consisted of tough plants that did well in the rich, moist soil. There were clumps of lupins; the giant purple-leaved *Ligularia* 'Desdemona' with its bright-orange 'daisy' sprays; shrubs such as our favourite mock orange, *Philadelphus* 'Belle Etoile', with large, purple-centred flowers, and white spiraea. Large-flowered lilacs and a weeping silver pear, *Pyrus salicifolia* 'Pendula', made a background to hydrangeas and to two rose-bushes grown as shrubs, 'Iceberg' and the Victorian 'Louise Odier'. At the other end of the border 'Felicia', a pink musk rose, accompanied the mock orange. Behind them grew the purple moss rose, 'William Lobb'. Here and there at the front of the border were planted dwarf azaleas in shades of pink. Daffodil bulbs were planted throughout the border. The main weed-suppressors, however, were the hardy dwarf geraniums—blue *Geranium grandiflorum* × 'A. T. Johnson', named for our old friend, the famous garden writer from Roewen, and also his variety of the pink *G. endressii*) the white *G. macrorrhizum*, the large, soft leaves of which give off a true rose-geranium scent; and a hybrid of the garden, possibly a cross between *G.* 'Russell Prichard' and *G. nodosum*, making excellent ground cover with dark green leaves and large purplish flowers that complement most other plants (see p. 37). This geranium drifted through the garden and we let it be: it was one of those happy accidents of nature. Wherever it seeded itself it seemed always to be in the right place, and the dense, foot-high cushion of leaves spread widely to keep down competing weeds. Without the hardy geraniums, our small garden would have needed much more constant maintenance, and we could not have left it with half such carefree minds. Important too, for anyone with a tidy mind, the taller of these geraniums, along with ligularia and day-lilies, helped to disguise fading daffodil foliage.

Similar principles have guided us in the planting of our new, small, bungalow garden in the Isle of Man. Weed-suppressors that we value are the dwarf periwinkles, the various forms of *Vinca minor*. Of these we have three blue-flowered varieties: *V. minor* 'Caerulea', that known as 'La Grave', and the double blue 'Multiplex'; also the double and single burgundy, though the double is shy to flower, and the white-blossomed, variegated form. It is impossible to fault their value as weed-suppressors but should the shade of overhead branches become too dense they will not flower freely. An open, sunny site suits them best and they should always be clipped over after flowering to keep their habit dense.

One danger that can occur when using ground-cover to keep down weeds is that of choosing a too rampant plant which, in its turn, becomes more trouble than the weeds. A classic example of this is the sweet-scented winter heliotrope, the *Petasites fragrans*, delightful along a woodland or streamside walk, but a plant which to us became a major garden menace when one tyro horticultural journalist was ill-advised enough to recommend it in a best-selling book. This emphasizes the importance of selecting the right plants for the right places when using underplanting to caretake a garden while the owner is away.

Correct plant choice and initial mulching care are essential to the success of a scheme which can be the happiest solution to the weed problem and at the same time a major factor in combating drought. By their own leaf-fall the carpeting plants constantly enrich the soil. Their three-fold action in suppressing weeds, conserving moisture and improving the soil structure can lead in the end to that absent gardener's Eldorado—the self-gardening border. So important a part does this action play in our programme that I shall devote much of the following chapters to its proper employments.

TWO

Combating Weeds and Offsetting Drought

Mulching of one kind or another is the absent gardener's best means to combat weeds and offset drought at the same stroke. As a technique, the use of the mulch goes back into gardening history. Basically it consists of covering the surface of the soil with a good layer of some suitable material with the purpose of conserving moisture, keeping down weeds, and/or protecting the flower or vegetable crops from dirt, and sometimes pests.

To ensure success, the ground to which a mulch is to be applied must first be cleared of all perennial weeds. Apart from that, it is important to mulch with the right materials (whether living, organic or manufactured) and to apply the mulch at the appropriate time of year—usually in spring when the soil has begun to warm up but is still moist.

Over the years a wide variety of materials has been used, ranging from such organic substances as straw, sawdust, bracken, and peat, to basic minerals like stones, gravel or sand, and recently to plastic manufactured substances. To these the flower gardener, and in particular the shrub gardener, has added the use of carpeting plants as a living mulch.

Correct mulching, by cutting down the evaporation from the soil due to the action of wind and sun, can much reduce the need for summer watering, thus enabling flowers, roses, shrubs and vegetables to thrive with only the intermittent attention that the absent or weekend gardener can give. The practice is of benefit to all gardeners, ensuring that the garden can take care of itself during holiday periods and any other absences from home.

Critics have sometimes argued that mulching results in surface rooting. This is to some extent true but it is not necessarily a bad thing, provided that the mulch is kept up. It is, in fact, helpful in that it ensures that the top few inches of soil (which otherwise dry out very speedily) will remain moist so that plant roots can make use of it. In hostile conditions, as on chalk where a root-frustrating hard pan often

exists within a few inches of the surface, mulching is especially beneficial in allowing the roots to make the most of the friable top soil
available. Plants will root up into the mulch and this can be very helpful when growing acid-preferring plants on neutral soil. With the aid
of a 15 cm (6 in) mulch of chopped green bracken we were able in a
former garden to grow choice rhododendrons and camellias in a clay
soil on the alkaline side of neutral. An acid grade of peat (pH 6–4·5) or
pulverized pine bark would have been equally suitable.

Some plants—the lily family in particular—use a mulch to the best
advantage by sending out stem roots into the material. This is of the
greatest benefit in allowing the plants to attain their maximum vigour.

Care must be taken in choosing mulching materials to ensure that
they are of a fairly open consistency through which water can percolate.
Close, dense mulches can mat on the soil surface, depriving the plants
of water and air and causing virtual suffocation. So important is it fully
to understand the advantages of the various popular mulches and the
techniques covering their correct use that I shall examine each one
separately.

Peat. Easily obtainable but apt to be expensive. It must be thoroughly
wetted by soaking before use. The easiest way to achieve this is (a) to
open the plastic bag and direct the hose-pipe trickle inside for some
minutes, before leaving the peat to absorb the water; or (b), with
smaller quantities, to punch holes in the bag and submerge it in a tub
or bath of water. Baled peat should receive several soakings from the
hose-pipe before use. It should be so wet that water can be squeezed
from each handful. Otherwise when spread over the ground it will
merely absorb rainwater and even the surface moisture from the soil,
releasing it to the air by evaporation and so completely defeating one of
the main objects of its use.

Providing this point is watched and a coarse grade is chosen, peat is a
first-rate mulching material. As it disintegrates it improves the soil
structure. If applied 10 cm (4 in) deep, it will effectively smother all
annual weeds and stifle the germination of any weed seedlings, while
not preventing the upward thrust of bulbs among shrubs or in a
flower border.

As with all organic mulches, the occasional weed seedling may root
into the mulch but this will easily be lifted out by hand or uprooted by
the hoe.

Grass clippings. These have the advantage of being easily obtained,
making a good, free, mulch for roses, shrubs or fruit trees, and to
use them in this way disposes of the lawn-mowing residue. The clip-

pings also compost well. However, they suffer from one or two dis-
advantages as a permanent mulching material, and I would always prefer
to limit their use to that of temporary expediency, as for instance when
one is unexpectedly going to be away and therefore unable to water, or
as a stand-by mulch for raspberries, the runner bean row or something
of this order.

Mowings from lawns that have recently been treated with weed-
killer should never be used either for mulching or composting. At least
six weeks must elapse after the last treatment before the clippings are
really safe to use.

Grass clippings tend to heat up considerably, so they must be kept
away from the stems of plants—on the other hand, the heat discourages
slugs and snails, which can be an advantage. Care should always be
taken not to apply too deep a layer; 5 cm (2 in) is ample. Being fine in
consistency, too thick a layer would mat and clog the soil. The clippings,
however, make a valuable contribution as they rot, adding humus and
improving the soil structure. Late in the season or when no better
mulching materials are to hand, it is wiser for the weekend gardener to
mulch with grass clippings than to leave the soil exposed to the ele-
ments.

Straw. Mulches of straw are loose and open in texture, permitting excellent rain penetration, and straw is first rate for mulching soft fruit or
vegetables. Its appearance is not attractive enough to recommend its
use in the flower garden.

Black plastic. A modern material, and a heavy grade proves first rate as
a mulch, but its use requires special techniques if its very qualities are
not to become detrimental. Forming an impervious barrier, it entirely
prevents evaporation from the soil. It also prevents the passage of
water to the soil. So in the vegetable garden it is wise to leave un-
covered strips on which the rain may fall between the plastic-mulched
rows. If laid flat, unperforated film may accumulate rainwater in the
hollows and this is not only wasteful but might cause the fruit or
vegetables to rot. To avoid such a situation, peas, beans, sprouts,
lettuces, strawberries, potatoes or any other subjects to be mulched
with the plastic should be planted on slight ridges off which the water
will run, thus irrigating the channels between.

When planting it is usual to lay the strips of plastic first and then to
plant through them, cutting crosses at each planting site, folding back
the edges and planting through the holes. This method also allows
the rain to trickle through to reach the roots of each plant.

A plastic mulch not only keeps down weeds and reduces the need
for watering, but it improves the soil structure and aeration by creating

warm, moist conditions which increase nitrification. There is less leaching of fertilizers, and fruit and vegetables do particularly well when a plastic mulch is used.

In the flower garden, black polythene may be laid down when planting a border—inserting the plants through the holes in the way described. To improve its appearance, gravel or pebbles should be laid over the surface of the plastic. This gives a Japanese effect and many pleasing textures can be achieved. Pebble beds of this type are virtually trouble-free, provided the ground is well enriched before planting. Charcoal should be added to the soil to keep it sweet.

Sawdust. These mulches have been used in Canada for many years with much success. As a mulching material, sawdust effectively suppresses weeds and as it rots helps to improve the soil. There are, however, certain points which must be watched if the greatest benefit is to be derived from its use.

As with a straw mulch, the wet soil tends to become compacted under it if the ground is trodden on, so one should keep off the plot except when strictly necessary. With shrubs or long-standing crops such as asparagus, soft fruit, globe artichokes etc, there is little need to venture on to the ground except to prune or to pick the crop. Three inches of sawdust will be sufficient to keep down weed germination in the flower border. The sawdust is long lasting and is an effective deterrent to slugs and snails.

The argument has often been raised that as the sawdust gradually breaks down and becomes incorporated in the soil, the organisms helping this process drain the soil of nitrogen. This is true, but the difficulty can be offset if extra nitrogen is applied. A spring dressing of nitro-chalk at the rate of about 34 g to 1 square metre (1 oz to 1 square yard) will set matters right and at the same time help to reduce any over-acidity in the sawdust.

During a hot summer, injury to some plants may arise because of the heat-reflective properties of such a mulch, but in most parts of Britain the chances of this happening are negligible, although in the hotter, south-eastern region it should be borne in mind.

Pulverized pine bark. This is an alternative to sawdust and has been used successfully on some of the borders in the Royal Horticultural Society's gardens at Wisley. Like sawdust, pine bark is readily available in forested areas and has the advantage that it is particularly attractive in appearance. So far no nitrogen deficiency seems to have resulted from its use.

Pine bark is exceptionally slow to break down and a 5 cm (2 in) layer will last for at least three years. Coarse in structure, it allows free percolation of rain and air, so—as it does not hold rain water in the way that peat does—there is loss by evaporation. Being heavier, it does not blow away as peat sometimes tends to in exposed areas. Pine bark not only repels slugs but mice as well—a great advantage in the protection of bulbs.

On herbaceous borders, the pine-bark mulch may be applied in autumn to prevent pest damage to such plants as delphiniums during spring.

The pH (acidity/alkalinity) of pine bark is low, around 5·5 indicating acidity, so it is ideal for mulching rhododendrons, heathers, other calcifuge plants and hydrangeas. On the other hand it may be a little too acid for some lime-lovers such as the dianthus family, clematis, some paeony species and hybrids, and some of the irises. It is a simple matter, however, to treat the ground surrounding the lime-lovers with ground limestone after the pine-bark mulch has become incorporated into the soil. The rate of application for this purpose may be calculated at roughly 0·5 to 1 kg per square metre (1 to 2 lb per square yard). One might also use nitro-chalk as recommended to offset nitrogen loss when using a sawdust mulch.

Certain doubts originally occurred as to whether the bark of some conifers might prove toxic, but all bark has now been found harmless, provided it is not used when too fresh. Suppliers usually stack their pulverized bark for about twelve weeks before delivery. When ordering it should be checked that this has been done.

The pulverized bark of many conifers has an ornamental effect that can be particularly pleasing in the flower borders or when used under shrubs or roses. For the best visual results the bark must be of a coarse grade—the fragments being up to 4 cm (1½ in) in diameter. The bark keeps its decorative effect for three years, after which it should be topped up. Differences of colour in the barks of various genera and species (mainly *abies* and *picea*) can be exploited to great effect by the gardener in the way that the Japanese use different-coloured, and shaped, stones to set off their plantings. For the week-end gardener who specializes in growing small shrubs and bulbs and lilies, and appreciates a tidy, 'gardened' effect even though he is away for much of the time, the use of conifer bark has a great deal to recommend it.

Those who do not live in forested areas can obtain a list of suppliers and retail stockists in various parts of the country from Bark Products (Bristol) Ltd, Netham Road, Bristol, BS5 9PQ. In addition the giant ICI group has now put on the market pulverized bark under the name 'Forest Bark' and this can be purchased from most nurseries and garden sundries shops.

Spent hops. These make a fine mulching material and are readily available in brewing areas; for example, Kent, Hereford and North Staffordshire. At Sissinghurst Castle in Kent they are used to mulch the famous garden of old-fashioned roses, as well as many of the borders. Each autumn they are forked into the ground and the mulch is renewed, so the hops not only suppress the weeds during the summer and prevent evaporation of the moisture in the soil, but they act as a very efficient fertilizer too.

Rather pale in colour and so not quite as visually effective as pulverized pine bark, spent hops are nevertheless a valuable weapon in the weekend gardener's armoury. They are readily obtainable from most breweries that use hops—not all do, these days.

One disadvantage is the unpleasant smell but this quickly dissappears once the mulch has been spread. Another—and this is also common to pulverized pine bark—is its attraction to birds which scratch in the mulch and tend to scatter it on to the grass and paths.

Green bracken. Easily come by in many hilly and mountainous areas of Britain. Cut green in June before the spores are ripe enough to effect its spread through the garden, it makes a splendid mulch for all shrubs and in particular for rhododendrons and members of the *Ericaceae*. It can be harvested with shears and then put through an old-fashioned chaff cutter of the type still to be obtained at many farm sales. Turning brown later, it is always harmonious in the garden and when used as a mulch it has an open texture that facilitates the passage of rain and can never clog.

Spent mushroom compost. This has the appearance of peat and is relatively cheap to buy, making a good mulch in the flower garden. As with all peats it should be thoroughly wetted before use. It is rather fine in texture and so should not be used at a greater depth than 5 cm (2 in). It is also alkaline-reacting and so not suitable for calcifuge plants of the *Ericaceae* type. Scattered over the herbaceous border or used to top-dress the stronger-growing non-calcifuge alpines it can help the absent gardener a great deal in his dual task of preventing evaporation and suppressing annual weeds.

Newspapers. Soaked in water and laid at the bottom of trenches and holes when planting, newspapers are helpful to soft fruit such as currants, raspberries and gooseberries; also to vegetables such as runner beans, and this method might be tried in the flower borders when setting out dahlias, sweet peas, and so on.

As a result of this survey, most gardeners will reach their own conclusions as to which organic or manufactured mulching materials suit their purpose best. It remains only to point two further guidelines. In these days of economic stress, it is obviously best to choose materials which are either free, relatively inexpensive, or else easily obtainable in your own district. Apart from this, it is important to suit the material to the purpose, as suggested in the following paragraphs.

For fruit and vegetables choose from straw, spent hops, mushroom compost (except for strawberries which prefer an acid medium), or black polythene, with grass-clippings as an ancilliary stop-gap.

For shrubs, pulverized pine bark would be my own choice, were expense not a primary consideration. Alternatively, where bracken is available use this chopped green in June and supplemented by rotted bracken detritus in autumn. A further alternative is to make Japanese-style pebble beds with black polythene, folding the plastic around established shrubs and replanting herbaceous material through specially cut holes.

For flower borders, use pulverized pine bark or sawdust (supplemented by nitro-chalk) or make pebble-bed features, covering the black polythene with pebbles or gravel.

Ground-cover addicts like myself will always prefer to use suitable plant material as a living mulch over much of the garden, limiting the use of other substances to that of expediency in keeping down weeds and preventing evaporation by mulching around the shrubs and ground-cover plants until the cover spreads and meets. For this purpose, wetted coarse peat, leaf-mould, rotted bracken, and pulverized pine bark are best, with the addition of spent hops and mushroom compost for all but lime-sensitive genera. Many of the ground-cover plants are comparatively expensive to buy in the first place, but yearly division and subsequent close-planting will help to increase the spread, while mulching techniques not only keep down weeds but improve the soil.

A list of the most effective weed-suppressing plants follows in the next chapter.

Though drought may to a great extent be overcome by the correct use of mulching materials, in extremely dry weather and in hot areas of the country the absent gardener may sometimes return to find that some of his plants are suffering. In our own garden we have returned from trips abroad to find rhododendrons with quilled and hanging leaves, and camellias in a partially defoliated state. In both instances, however, the mulches had prevented total drying out so that, with the administration of a thorough soaking, the rhododendrons quickly recovered. The camellias (which have a less satisfactory method of adapting themselves to resist evaporation by controlling the demeanour of their leaves, and so had suffered more) were cut back, removing the top foot or so of growth which seemed to have suffered most. They subsequently recovered, made new leaves and by the following summer had quite made up the lost ground.

To prevent tragedies occurring, drain-pipes could be sunk at strategic points near by, filled with a few inches of soil and a few inches of pebbles, then topped from time to time with water which is released to the soil gradually at a depth where it will form a reservoir on which the plant roots can draw. This type of concentrated watering helps particularly with precious plants and with subjects such as hydrangeas which are quickly affected by hot sun, but the method would be impracticable to use over the garden as a whole.

One might also consider the establishing of a system of sprinklers operated by an easily accessible outside tap which a kindly neighbour might be willing to turn on, leaving the water running for an hour or two and then returning to turn the tap off again.

However, in times of water shortage, by far the best method is the use of deep mulches, laid when the soil is moist after rain, and before the drying winds of spring have done their worst.

THREE

A Dictionary of Ground Cover

Not only does the use of efficient ground-covering plants suppress weeds but it also helps to reduce evaporation from the soil. To be effective, the leaf-spread of the plants must touch, because it is only by the exclusion of light that weed germination can be prevented and the growth of existing undesirables stifled.

Ground-cover plants, like all others, are expensive to buy these days. Some genera may, admittedly, be raised from seed but this is a process that is often impossible for the weekend or otherwise regularly absent gardener. One is limited, therefore, to buying what one can afford at the time and patiently building up one's stock by offsets, layering-in-situ, or the removal and replanting of suckers. Fortunately many suitable subjects lend themselves to this type of increase. The hardy geranium, ivy, pernettya, ajuga, astilbe and hypericum are genera that at once come to mind. Others, like the hellebore, readily seed, and if one watches for the seedlings while weeding one has to hand a free ready-made stock. Some plants such as the lungworts (*Pulmonaria* species), hostas and so on, form large clumps which can be regularly divided and replanted at the requisite distances to increase the spread.

Some ground-covering plants do best in drifts of their own kind. Others may be intermingled with plants that like similar conditions to form a 'commune', as suggested in the following pages.

If weed-suppressing plants are to fulfil their function properly, it is vital that they should be set in absolutely clean ground. While they are becoming established, and until continuous cover is achieved, they should be assisted by mulching the ground between with peat, pine bark, chopped bracken or even polythene.

In the list that follows, stars have been awarded to denote the efficiency with which the plants perform their task. Heights are stated when they exceed 30 cm (1 ft).

** **Ajuga reptans**. In its green form this is a prolifically spreading bugle which succeeds in shade or sun and bears the sturdy blue flower spikes of its family. The red-leafed form, 'Rubra', is less reliable in hot, dry soil but gives good, low, ground cover in good soil in shade. Both are suitable to use at the forefront of the shrub or flower border or to underplant roses. Set 20 cm (8 in) apart.

** **Alchemilla mollis.** The favourite lady's mantle has beautiful pleated, rounded downy leaves above which rises an airy display of yellow-green feathery stars. It is a plant of great garden effect, reaching a height of 45 cm (18 in). Used alone it will form close and effective ground cover at the forefront of shrubs, or it may be planted in a border 'commune' where it associates well with *Salvia officinalis* 'Purpurescens' (the common purple-leafed sage), *Stachys lanata*, with its grey silky lamb's ear foliage, and white or blue columbines, to give dense weed-suppressing cover, at the same time forming a most attractive colour grouping. Set 30 cm (1 ft) apart for quick results.

** **Anaphalis triplinervis** (see p. 80).

* **Anemone hupehensis.** The original Japanese anemone of September gardens is an excellent ground-covering plant for use either in the border or among shrubs, growing to 60–90 cm (2–3 ft). *A. vitifoila* is more free-spreading, a determined colonizer that will quickly give dense leaf coverage over a large area (see also p. 80). The leaves are wide, vine-like and dull green and make a good foil for the dusty pink flowers. Both it and the white *A. hupehensis* 'Alba' do best where the soil is not too dry. Large colonies can be easily established to give effective summer ground cover and delightful autumn flowers reaching 60 cm (2 ft) in height. Set 45 cm (18 in) apart.

*** **Anthemis cupaniana** is a wonderful weed-suppressor for well-drained soils in full sun. Coming from Italy, it may not be fully hardy in all areas and some authorities state that it needs annual division. With us, in North Wales (and to within eight miles of the sea) it looked after itself entirely. It yields numerous offspring and roots as it goes, forming wide, dense mats of silvery-grey foliage above which rises an embroidery of pure white, gold-centred 'daisies'. For a sunny slope in light soil it cannot be bettered. Set 45 cm (18 in) apart.

* **Aquilegia alpina.** The columbine is perfect to grow in a ground-cover 'commune'. Attractive in its own right, especially in the 'Hensol Harebell' strain with its deep Wedgwood-blue colouring, it seeds freely and does well in sun or shade in any soil.

* **Arisarum proboscideum.** The mouse-tail plant is a novelty that intrigues most children and adults, as well as doing a fair ground-covering job as it spreads. Happy in sun or shade, it does best where the ground is not too dry, yielding increasing hummocks of low, glossy spear-

shaped leaves through which project small purplish-white arum-like flowers with 13 cm (5 in) maroon-purple 'tails', for all the world like tiny floral mice. Perhaps one should not really include it among weed-suppressors, but nevertheless over the years it builds up into a good ground cover that smothers annual weed germination. Possibly it should best be looked on as a weekend gardener's 'fun plant' that is also a long-term investment with eventual ground-cover growth yield.

** **Artemisia canescens.** A foliage plant of the wormwood family that gives dense ground cover, it is freely branching and makes a mass of lacy divided leaves on ascending stems. Three or four plants set at intervals (they reach a height of 45 cm (18 in)) would make an interesting and beautiful addition to a ground-cover 'commune'. It can also be used in the flower border or among shrub roses. Set 45 cm (18 in) apart.

*** **Astilbe × arendsii.** The feathery-plumed hybrid astilbes in their various colours of crimson, rose, shrimp, lilac and cream make most efficient weed-suppressors for difficult wet soils. They also help to mop up surplus moisture in persistently wet or weedy corners and 'garden' a streamside or pool. Good named forms are the dark-crimson 'Fanal', 'Betsy Cuperus' in clear pink, 'Salmon Queen', 'Hyacinth' in lilac, and the white 'Deutschland'. Set originally at 45 cm (18 in) apart they quickly form strong mats, and after two or three years may be divided and the offsets used to colonize a larger area. All those mentioned grow from 75 to 90 cm (2½ to 3 ft) high.

There is also the dwarf *A. simplicifolia* which spreads rapidly, but not by any means uncontrollably, in moist sunny soil. This is a useful plant to associate with *Campanula portenschlagiana* (*muralis*), *Polygonum affine*, alyssum, dianthus and so on, in a trouble-free ribbon border of easy alpines.

*** **Ballota pseudodictamnus.** This plant, which comes from Crete, forms mounds of trailing and erect stems attractively set with pale-grey, rounded woolly leaves reaching a height of 45 cm (18 in). Its flowers are small, lavender pink and (although flower arrangers like them) have little impact in the garden scene. I find it best to shear them off, which results in keeping the plants low and spreading and helps to make them even more effective at their job of keeping down weeds. Treated like this each plant will cover a square metre (just over a square yard) when established. They are effective at the front of the flower border and in the forefront of shrubs on a sunny bank or they can be used in a 'commune' of similar sun-loving subjects. Set 45 to 60 cm (18 in to 2 ft) apart.

*** **Bergenia.** The delight of many flower arrangers and no less useful in the weekend gardener's portfolio of weed-defeating stock, as their large, leathery, mainly evergreen leaves suppress all weed growth. They will adapt to any soil and can be used in sun or shade, although in full sun and sharply drained ground their leaves will colour magnificently during the winter months, yielding an especial bonus in the way of foliage to take back for the flower vases in town. From an original planting 30 cm (1 ft) apart, after two or three seasons the clumps will be ready to divide so as to increase the area covered. If left alone, within five years each individual plant will spread to cover a patch about a metre (1 yard) wide. Apart from the common *B. cordifolia*, the purple-leafed *B. c.* 'Purpurea' and the newer white-flowered 'Schneelicht' are worth growing. Flower arrangers may favour the hybrid 'Ballawley' ('Delbees') beeause of the peculiar leaden-liver colour of its foliage in winter, but in my experience this variety is not so hardy nor such a good 'doer' as the other forms. Set 30 to 60 cm (1 to 2 ft) apart.

* **Borago laxiflora.** This member of the borage family makes good ground cover in good soil. From hairy, low-growing rosettes, summer trails of tiny, light blue Chinaman's-hat type of flowers appear. It frequently colonizes by self-sown seed. Set 25 cm (10 in) apart for quick effect.

* **Brunnera macrophylla.** A fair weed-suppressor in rich soil, its spread varies very much in relation to the ground in which it is grown. It is worth growing for its sprays of sky-blue 'forget-me-nots' on 45 cm (18 in) stems, but its value to the weekend gardener is in direct ratio to the soil he can offer. Set 23 cm (9 in) apart.

** **Buphthalmum speciosum.** This plant bears orange-yellow 'daisy' flowers reminiscent of a rather small inula and grows to over 60 cm (2 ft) in height. Its value lies in its large coarse leaves which make good ground cover. Set 45 to 60 cm (18 in to 2 ft) apart.

Calluna (ling). Unfortunately the lings do not make such satisfactory weed-suppressors as do some of the ericas. They are most attractive, however, and will be found in Chapter Five—Long-Season Performers.

** **Campanula portenschlagiana.** This is a mauve-purple harebell with a tough dwarf habit and dense leafage—formerly known as *C. muralis*. It spreads easily, may be divided each season and makes good ground cover under roses, at the front of a border or to fill in paving cracks. It is not to be confused with the rampant starry-flowered *C. poscharsk-yana*, mauvish blue (and its white variety 'E. H. Frost'), which, though a weed in many places, can nevertheless render the absent gardener yeoman service by covering yards of ground in rough places where its invasiveness can be looked on as an asset. *C. portenschlagiana* is dense enough to smother many weeds, grass seedlings occasionally take root in it but are quite easily removed. It is especially important to make sure that the ground is clear of all couch grass before planting. Set 25 cm (10 in) apart.

*** **Cistus.** Though not hardy in all areas, these make first-rate weed-suppressing shrubs in sunny, well-drained spots and at the seaside, reaching a height of 60 to 120 cm (2 to 4 ft), though the excellent *C. laurifolius* may grow rather taller. They may be grown in variety to cover a problem bank or mixed with other sun-lovers such as *Phlomis fruticosa*, *Viburnum tarreri* (fragrans) (to give height and winter fragrance), rosemary, lavender, santolina, *Senecio greyi* and hebes such as 'Great Orme' and 'Midsummer Beauty'. Among the hardiest are *Cistus × corbariensis* with crimson-tinted buds opening to crinkly white sun-roses; *C. lusitanicus* 'Decumbens', which forms a low mound covered with crimson-blotched white blooms: the 'Silver Pink' with long clusters of crumpled pink salvers; and *C. creticus* with very grey foliage that gains a pinkish tinge from its stems and carries delightful mauve-pink flowers. Set 1·5 m (5 ft) apart.

* **Convallaria majalis.** The lily of the valley will not grow in all places and was a failure in our previous Welsh garden. Notoriously temperamental, it prefers semi-shade and a degree of moisture in the soil. Dry ground or too much shade are factors that prevent its establishment. However, it is worth trying, not only for its fragrant and beautiful flowers in May, but because its long-lasting leaves make weed-proof ground cover where it is content enough to colonize. Set 15 cm (6 in) apart.

*** **Cotoneaster dammeri.** This prostrate evergreen shrub is ideal for covering banks, or making ground cover beneath lightly branched taller subjects. Its sealing-wax-red berries are prolific in autumn and add greatly to its attraction, while its glossy small leaves make dense ground cover. Set 60 cm (2 ft) apart.

*** **Crocosmia masonorum.** In appearance akin to the old-fashioned montbretia and to the more spectacular antholyza, this densely spreading corm-rooted plant that makes effective cover in milder districts. With us in North Wales there was never any problem or query about its hardiness so I was surprised to read in Mr Alan Bloom's useful *Perennials for Trouble-Free Gardening* (Faber) that he lists it as 'of doubtful hardiness except in milder districts' and recommends lifting and storing in peat during the winter months. Mr Bloom is a leading grower and an acknowledged expert on hardy plants, so for colder areas one should follow his advice and stick to the former montbretia, now officially *Crocosmia crocosmiiflora*, which will smother the weeds with its copious bright-green leaves that offset the sprays of orange, tiny gladiolus-like flowers. Where it will 'do', *C. masonorum* is much more effective in flower, with 75 cm (2½ ft) arching sprays of more brilliant bloom. Set 15 cm (6 in) apart.

*** Cynara cardunculus. The cardoons or their near relative *C. scolymus*, the globe artichoke, are among the most handsome of strikingly architectural plants and at the same time fulfil the useful function of suppressing all weeds for quite a wide area. Growing to a height of 1·2 to 1·5 m (4 to 5 ft) with immense thistle heads and deeply divided, recurving silver-grey leaves they make a magnificent border feature. Each plant will quite soon cover about a square metre (square yard) or more. Not fully hardy in the coldest areas, they should be planted in spring in a warm, sunny, well-drained position where once established they will quickly go ahead. *C. scolymus* differs mainly from its distinguished relative in that its leaves are not quite so grey and its flowers are not prickly. Nevertheless it is an extremely handsome plant in its own right and to my mind worth including in any weekend garden for the bonus of its delicious vegetable yield. Set 90 cm to 1·2 m (3 to 4 ft) apart.

** Dianthus. Of the many species and forms of carnation and pink family, the most trouble-free are the Highland Hybrids which form tussocks of grey foliage a foot or more across and seem to thrive endlessly in any sunny well-drained soil without division. They are first rate for planting under roses to keep down weeds. Set 30 cm (1 ft) apart.

*** Dimorphotheca barberiae. This plant is now officially known as *Osteospermum jucundum*, but as dimorphotheca is the name by which most people still know it in its native South Africa and is certainly the name by which it is usually referred to by those who grow it, I have used the familiar designation. Hardy in a sunny, well-drained position, this is a first-rate plant for keeping down weeds in a dryish border. Each plant makes rounded tussocks of greenery about 45 cm (18 in) across, from which rise pleasing mauve-pink, silver-backed daises on 15 cm (6 in) stalks for months on end. Its fellow, *D. ecklonensis*, with white, blue-zoned daises has two forms—one taller-growing (up to 60 cm (2 ft)) which is less hardy, and one which makes even wider mats than *D. barberae* and is just as hardy and accommodating. Set 45 cm (18 in) apart.

*** Epimedium. There are several species of this beautiful and useful genus which make weed-impenetrable ground cover, and it is only their initial cost and comparative slowness to increase that prevents their wider use. Provided one is content to start off with three or four plants and to split them up each season, mulching between them to defeat weeds until the gaps are closed, they are a worthwhile addition to the absent gardener's plant list. I could not claim, however, that

B

they are a help in conserving moisture. Preferring a damp, rich soil themselves, they will nonetheless adapt to poor conditions, but when they do so they extract so much from the soil as to impoverish it for competitors (including weeds, which is a bonus). *E. grandiflorum* 'Rose Queen' is the loveliest, carrying in early spring flights of deep pink to light crimson flowers like tiny columbines. *E. perralderanum* is one of the best for ground-cover purposes, with large, glossy, evergreen leaves that take on bright tints in autumn and winter. Its yellow flowers look well with cynoglossum or brunnera. To ensure the best flowers, leave the plants their protection of dead leaves in winter but remove them as soon as the flowers are over. Division to increase the stock is best carried out in autumn. Set 30 to 45 cm (1 ft to 18 in) apart.

*** **Erica carnea.** The attractive winter-flowering heath varies in its efficiency as ground cover according to the cultivar chosen. With us, *E.c.* 'Springwood' is undoubtedly the best, spreading quickly and (provided the plants are sheared over after flowering) making dense weed-smother. Its pure white, tan-anthered flowers are a bonus from January until March. The only drawback, to some people, is the fact that its flowers are white, resembling drifts of snow at a somewhat chilly season. This can be offset by including patches of *E.c.* 'Sprinwood Pink' or the taller, lilac *E.* × *darleyensis* in the planting. On light, stony soils in full sun, so long as the ground has been well cleared of weeds, one can make mixed plantings of all the heaths, and gain delightful year-round foliage and flower effect. Where lime is present, however, only the *E. carnea* forms and *E. mediterranea, E.* × *darleyensis, E. ciliaris* and possibly *E. vagans* (see following paragraph) will survive. The *Calluna* cultivars (ling) and the *E. cinerea* (bell heather) forms need an acid growing medium. None do well in shallow, chalk soils where it would be better to choose other ground-covering plants. *E. carnea* '*Springwood*' should be set at 45 cm (18 in) apart, other *carneas* at 25 cm (10 in) apart.

*** **Erica vagans.** In neutral or acid soils, this is another three-star plant. Taller-growing, the Cornish heath bears in summer bottle-brush spikes in shades of pink or rose. 'Mrs D. F. Maxwell' is the best in flower, with handsome raspberry-rose bottle-brushes. Its dark-green foliage makes dense ground cover. Like the winter heath, *E. vagans* should be well clipped over after flowering. Set 60 cm (2 ft) apart.

*** **Eryngium.** At least one species of sea holly, the Mexican *E. eburneum* (*bromeliifolium*), is spreading and persistent enough to be used for our purpose. Its 1·2 m (4 ft) stems bear clusters of small, pale-green thistly heads with white stamens, rendering it beautiful as well as useful. It gradually forms wide mats of narrow evergreen leaves, if given a sunny position in well-drained soil. It is ideal for a trouble-free bed composed of effective, self-gardening plants. *E. maritimum*, our native sea holly, is also attractive with its spiny glaucous leaves and blue thistly heads. If massed, it will form well-clothed, weed-free stretches in hot, dry sandy soils and is most useful to the weekend gardener who gardens by the sea. *E. eburneum* should be planted at 45 to 60 cm (18 in to 2 ft) apart, while the native *E. maritimum* needs closer spacing at 30 cm (1 ft) intervals. Heights range from 60 to 120 cm (2 to 4 ft) according to species.

*** **Euphorbia.** Two of the spurges make effective weed-smother, as well as being striking and attractive plants. *E. epithymoides* colours after the daffodils are over, providing a similar tone of bright yellow with a tinge of green. Liking a sunny spot, it forms a rounded dome with round, flat yellow heads of bracts. Plants of this species should be set about 30 cm (1 ft) apart.

E. wulfenii is considerably larger and not recommended for very small gardens—one plant covering a square metre (about a square yard) of ground and suppressing all weeds. It is also one of the most effective garden plants, sometimes growing to a height of some 1·2 m (4 ft) with handsome glaucous leaves, topped in spring with showy heads of bright lemon-green bloom, beloved of flower arrangers. Happy in any soil, it should be planted where it is protected from buffeting winds which might break off the long, leafy shoots.

*** **Fatshedera lizei.** A cross between fatsia, the misleadingly named castor oil plant, and hedera, ivy. It combines the best facets of both, bearing large, leathery palmate leaves similar to those of the fatsia, and having a spreading, floppy habit that smothers all weeds. Shade-tolerant, able to thrive in all soils, impervious to salt or to atmospheric pollution, it is everyman's dream ground cover. Eventually decorating a wide area, it is a splendid plant to clothe an awkward bank. It is also effective enough to be used decoratively in a pebble-bed, planted through the black polythene used as a mulch and being most effectively set off by the texture of small stones designed to disguise the plastic.

*** **Gaultheria procumbens.** This must have a lime-free soil; then it is one of the best evergreen carpeters, and does well under shrubs or in moist, woodland soils. This creeping wintergreen has shiny dark, small leaves that justify its common name by their aromatic scent. The plants bear pinky-white flower bells in spring, to be followed by long-lasting crimson berries that nestle in the leafy carpet of their foliage. It forms a dense, weed-proof ground mantle. The plants should be set about 45 cm (18 in) apart. If top-dressed they will layer themselves to give a ready means of increase.

*** **Genista hispanica.** The Spanish gorse is a dense, 60 cm (2 ft) high, spreading carpeter that can be relied on to carry out first-rate weed-suppression. Sheared over after flowering, it can be kept low and thick. Becoming a sheet of gold in spring, it is also of considerable floral value. A public garden in our locality combines it with *Hypericum calycinum* (see p. 39) with good effect. The gold of the gorse is set off by the fresh green of the hypericum's new leaves, and the golden rose of Sharon bowls in summer continue the colour note. Thus two long spells of bloom are obtained from the one planting. The technique is to drift the two genera through each other in the pattern of five plants of hypericum to five of the genista, thus:

$$+\ + \qquad \times \times \times \qquad +\ +$$
$$+ + + \qquad \times\ \times \qquad + + +$$

at 60 cm (2 ft) intervals.

*** **Geranium** (hardy species). Several of the true geraniums, as against greenhouse pelargoniums (regal, ivy-leaf and zonals), are the finest weed-suppressors I know. In our own garden the pink *G. endressii* 'A. T. Johnson' carries its bright pink blooms above 30 cm (1 ft) high hummocks of light-green divided foliage. Each plant covers about a 45 cm (18 in) square of ground during the summer months, dying back to a basal tuft during the winter. Often the species will seed itself and it is capable also of rapid propagation by division of the clumps.

G. *grandiflorum* 'Alpinum' covers still greater area with its rather lax, leafy stems. Its flowers are even more attractive than those of *G. endressii*, salver-shaped and of a lovely blue, beautifully veined with crimson. In autumn its leaves turn to shades of scarlet and crimson before dying back to the basal tuft. One plant will initially cover an area 1·9 m (2 sq ft) but in subsequent years this will increase to a square metre (a square yard or more). As with *G. endressii*, the clumps can be divided and the divisions will settle down quickly. There is also the twice-flowering 'Johnson's Blue'.

We find *G. macrorrhizum* is the most efficient ground-covering geranium of all. Quickly spreading, each initial clump soon covers an area 1·2 m (4 ft) or more wide, rooting as it goes and yielding many off-shoots for division. The leaves of this species are large and softly hairy, giving off a true rose-geranium scent when disturbed. The flowers of *G.m.* 'Album' are white and individually quite small, but create a flowery effect in the garden because they are so freely borne. The red calyces give the flowers a pinkish tinge. The type bears soft-pink flowers.

There are other geranium species, most of which are useful as ground cover, but the above are by far the most efficient weed-suppressors.

The hardy geraniums yield self-sown seedlings easily and so naturalize themselves throughout the garden. There is also the chance of hybrids occcurring. One of these which inhabits our own garden has dense, dark green foliage, making wide, 45 to 60 cm (18 in to 2 ft) high clumps of foliage, which contrast well with the lighter leaves of the various species. It bears light magenta-purple flowers which have an attraction of their own.

Thriving on almost any soils, the hardy geraniums go a long way to cutting down the work of weeding, and will give the plot of any 'absent' gardener a cared-for, thoughtfully planted look.

*** **Gunnera manicata.** A statuesque giant for marshy, wet ground or for use at the waterside, it will suppress all weeds. It has a definite function as ground cover for wet areas in large gardens. Each leaf measures about 1·7 m (6 ft) across, and the plant has considerable landscape effect, reaching to 90 cm (3 ft) or more and forming dense clumps.

*** **Hedera helix.** *H. h.* 'Hibernica', the Irish ivy, is a fine ground cover for rough ground and will throttle any weeds but care must be taken to prevent it climbing into shrubs and trees.

On a smaller scale any of the native ivies may be used, and one might include some of the charming variegated or gold-leafed types. 'Buttercup' has an entirely yellow leaf, while 'Gold Heart' ('Jubilee') has dark green leaves with golden centres. My friend, the late Mrs Margery Fish—who wrote many books on garden plants—always claimed that 'Jubilee' coloured better in shade, but I find that the leaves tend to become plain green in dense shade but retain their gold centres in a lighter place.

The silver-variegated 'Silver Queen' is good where only a small area is to be covered, but for larger spaces the silver-and-white 'Glacier' is a better choice. All increase rapidly and rooted stems can be removed to extend the planting.

For rough places the far more vigorous *H. colchica* 'Paddy's Pride' (obtainable from Hilliers) is an impressive variegated variety with large glossy leaves centrally splashed with yellow. It is much hardier than the beautiful *H. canariensis* 'Gloire de Marengo' with cream, silvery-grey and white variegations. This latter, however, is the most beautiful ivy of all and makes good ground cover near the sea. It succeeded well with us in North Wales.

*** **Helleborus orientalis** hybrids. These Lenten roses are true dual-purpose plants, affording exciting winter bloom followed by densely handsome leaf cover (at about 45 cm (18 in) up to 60 cm (2 ft) from the ground) which will successfully prevent weed germination. They may be raised from seed but it will take three years to produce sizeable flowering plants. Bought plants should be set 45 cm (18 in) apart and will rapidly give good cover. The bowl-shaped flowers come in variations of white, greenish-white, pink, peach, maroon and purple, often intriguingly speckled with purple or crimson. The blooms last well when cut provided the stalks are slit for 7 cm (3 in) before being plunged to the neck in warm water.

*** **Hemerocallis.** The day lilies are good flowering plants which again afford dense ground cover. Established clumps reach a height of 75 to 90 cm (2½ to 3 ft) and will occupy about ·19m² (about 2 sq ft) of ground and they should be planted at that distance. I find them particularly useful under shrubs or in the mixed border where their foliage will overlay and help to disguise the dying foliage of any nearby daffodils.

* **Heuchera.** Bressingham Hybrids make attractive ground cover at the front of a border or in small patches at the forefront of shrubs. They succeed only in well-drained, good soil. After a few years the crowns tend to emerge above the soil and they must then have a covering of light soil worked in around them to encourage new roots to form. Alternatively they should be divided and replanted every three or four years, which also helps to increase the stock. Only those crowns with good fibrous roots should be retained, and these should be planted deeply so that they will not work themselves out of the ground too quickly. Division should take place in spring or September.

Heucherella. Similar to heuchera, but a more dwarf and compact plant, though *H. tiarelloides* is often recommended by connoisseurs as ground cover, it is subject to the same limitations as the heucheras and so is not really a plant on which the absent gardener can rely. Set 30 cm (1 ft) apart.

** **Hosta.** Beloved of flower arrangers for their foliage, these are pleasant in the garden throughout the season; in spring the leaves are at their best, and in summer the liliaceous spikes of mauve appear. The genus makes really effective ground cover with first-rate weed-suppressing properties. It receives only two stars because the foliage is rather late to emerge, towards the end of May, and because it is often subject to slug depradations which mar its beauty. Any of the species are good, but among the most vigorous are *H. fortunei* 'Gigantea' with extra large leaves and 75 cm (2½ ft) flower spikes, *H. plantaginea* and the wavy-leafed *H. undulata*. Lovers of variegated foliage will appreciate *H. albomarginata* with creamy leaf edges, and *H. fortunei* 'Albopicta', the spring leaves of which are butter yellow edged with pale green. The colouring fades to an all-over green as summer progresses. Set 60 cm (2 ft) apart.

** **Hydrangea petiolaris.** When grown prostrate, the climbing hydrangea makes excellent ground cover for large areas in poor soil, one plant covering a large area. It is particularly useful because it will do well in shade. Although it loses its leaves in winter, its summer foliage cover is dense enough to suppress all weeds, while its flowers are like those of the lace cap hydrangeas.

*** **Hypericum calycinum.** The rose of Sharon receives full marks for week suppression. It will grow almost anywhere, however poor the soil, and does well in sun or shade. Clipped over after flowering, it remains dense and tidy. As suggested on p. 36 it can be combined with the Spanish gorse (*Genista hispanica*) to give an attractive two-shaded ground cover with two seasons of flowering. Set 60 cm (2 ft) apart.

** **Iberis sempervivens.** The perennial white-flowered candytuft if sheared flowering will give dense weed-suppressing cover. The greatest danger to its effectiveness is couch-grass which may invade from outside the clumps or may grow from rhizomes missed when cleaning the ground. As with most ground-covering plants, its success depends on the ground being absolutely weed-free before planting. Set 60 cm (2 ft) apart.

*** **Juniperus conferta.** One of the best low-growing ground covers among this most useful genus, it will grow in alkaline or acid conditions and has a branch cover that smothers anything. The foliage of this species is bright green and prickly. Specimens should be set 60 cm (2 ft) apart initially. The plants may later be moved to a wider spacing as they spread. I like to make a tapestry of different foliage colours and heights, weaving in this juniper along with the blue-grey *J. horizontalis* forms, the dark green *J. communis* 'Repanda' and *J.* × *media* 'Pfitzerana Aurea' which needs to have its ascending branches removed as it grows, so that it does not become out of character with the others.

*** **Lamium galeobdolon 'Variegatum'.** I include this here because it makes a most effective ground-covering trailer, embroidering the ground between shrubs or at the base of a rough hedge, helping to keep down weeds and at the same time being wonderfully decorative with its soft-green, white-painted leaves and handsome spikes of soft-yellow flowers. It is evergreen. In three years one plant will cover quite a large area and yield many offshoots, rooted from trailers as it spreads.

*** **Lamium maculatum.** This makes a lower, less invasive carpet. Like its more rampant relation it will grow almost anywhere but does best where the ground is not too dry. The type has pinkish-purple flowers; the white and pink flowered forms are much less reliable but make effective ground cover in good conditions. All have pretty sage-green leaves striped with white and often tinged with pink. There is another species, *L. orvala*, which is more like the typical dead-nettle in growth and which makes handsome clumps of soft green foliage reaching 45 cm (18 in) in height. The type has pinky-claret flowers that are very attractive in mass and there is a white form which is even more showy. Set *L. maculatum* 30 cm (1 ft) apart; *L. orvala* 45 cm (18 in) apart.

** **Ligularia** 'Desdemona'. A handsome border plant, in moist soil this makes a fine weed-suppressor, growing to a height of 90 cm (3 ft). It has fine purple-backed leaves and stems and branching sprays of showy orange 'daisy' flowers. It may be massed in boggy ground to help absorb surplus water. Set 90 cm (3 ft) apart.

*** **Lysichitum americanum.** One of the best weed-suppressors for boggy ground or for a streamside, the bog arum reaches a height of 45 cm (18 in). Its huge paddle-shaped leaves are very showy and in spring it bears quantities of bright gold, large arum-type flowers. *L. camtchatcense* has even finer blue-grey foliage and white flowers with gold spadices. Set 90 cm (3 ft) apart.

*** **Mahonia aquifolium.** This shrub, together with the more dwarf *nervosa* (the latter is said not to be at best on chalk), makes fine ever-green ground cover dense enough to keep down all weeds. Known to most gardeners, they bear attractive, compound, holly-like leaves and stubby upright racemes of mustardy flowers in spring. They grow to 60 to 90 cm (2 to 3 ft) and should be set 90 cm (3 ft) apart.

Montbretia, see *Crocosmia*.

** **Origanum vulgare** 'Aureum'. The golden marjoram has leaves which can be used in cooking. It makes dense mats in sunny places in well-drained soil and may best be used to form a 'commune', planting in company with *Anthemis cupaniana*, *Artemisia canescens*, some of the sages or other sun-lovers. Set 30 cm (1 ft) apart.

Osteospermum jucundum, see *Dimorphotheca barberiae*.

*** **Pachysandra terminalis.** This is much used in America and can be equally helpful here, colonizing poor, dry ground under trees and shrubs where little else will grow. There is a pleasingly marked form with creamy-white edges, known as 'Variegata'. Set 45 cm (18 in) apart.

*** **Pernettya.** This evergreen, berrying genus (which grows to 60 cm (2 ft)) makes fine weed-suppressing cover for acid soil, but it can be invasive so its use should be restricted to places where good dense 'boskage' is needed to form a large colony, perhaps under trees, to surround large shrubs, or to 'garden' tracts of sandy, healthy soil. If the Davis Hybrids are planted, a good variety of berries will result—crimson, pink, puce and white. Set 60 cm (2 ft) apart.

*** **Phlomis.** This is a genus offering at least one fine weed-suppressing shrub for sunny places in the species, *P. fruticosa*, the Jerusalem sage, which is distinctive with its grey-green leaves and strikingly whorled bright yellow flower heads. Surprisingly hardy, this Mediterranean shrub does well in all but the coldest areas and associates well with other sun-lovers to make efficient and attractive permanently 'gardened' plantings, growing to a height of 90 cm (3 ft) and occupying an area 1·2 m (4 ft) square.

*** **Potentilla.** Deciduous, but not particular as to soil, the potentillas of the *fruticosa* group, notably *P. f. arbuscula*, will, if clipped over after flowering, form dense, spreading ground cover at a height of about 60 cm (2 ft). They bloom from May to October. Set 90 cm (3 ft) apart.

*** **Pulmonaria.** Among the most reliable of the herbaceous ground-covering genera, this plant has large weed-suppressing leaves that 'flop' to cover a wide area. *P. rubra*, the rosy-pink Christmas cowslip, is the best at its task. Slightly later to emerge and flowering in spring, the blue-flowered *P. angustifolia* (syn. *P. azurea*) is also good, but with us the spotted-leafed *P. saccharata*—the soldiers and sailors lungwort—is less reliable. In my experience it needs a moister soil and full or partial shade to do well. The other two species are much less fussy. Set 60 cm (2 ft) apart.

*** **Rodgersia.** This genus makes first-rate leaf-cover at a height of 90 cm (3 ft) in marshy, wet ground or at the waterside. The plants do well in sun or partial shade and are handsome whether in flower or leaf. Their palmate foliage is extremely broad and noble-looking, making them fine plants in their own right. *R. pinnata* 'Superba' is one of the best having deep rose plumes, while *R. tabularis* has plumes of creamy white and those of *R. aesculifolia* from creamy white to pale pink. Set 60 cm (2 ft) apart.

*** **Rosmarinus lavendulaceus (prostratus).** This plant is not fully hardy in all areas but near the sea and in warm, sloping southern gardens it makes splendid ground cover either on its own or in association with a 'commune' of maquis-type planting. Set 60 cm (2 ft) apart.

*** **Ruta graveolens.** Rue—especially in its form 'Jackman's Blue'—is a wonderful, ground-covering, foliage plant for hot, sunny spots. Ideal for use in a 'commune' of plants enjoying similar conditions it makes dense hummocky bushes reaching a height of 60 to 90 cm (2 to 3 ft) covered with a lacework of finely divided grey-blue leaves. Best of all, it is evergreen. A drift of several bushes worked in with prostrate rosemary, phlomis, tree lupin, nepeta, *Stachys lanata*, cistus and some of the hebes can render any sunny, well-drained place attractively weed-free in perpetuity. We have a bank of these in our garden and the only attention it needs is an occasional pruning when some of the plants begin to overlap. (Both the nepeta and the *Stachys lanata* do better for the removal of flowered stems.) Set 60 cm (2 ft) apart.

*** **Salvia officinalis.** The common sage makes excellent ground cover in hot, dry places or for almost any sunny spot in well-drained soil. Try, to get, if you can the English broad-leafed form which seldom flowers but forms a dense, shrubby hummock about 45 cm (18 in) high. It is effectively worked in with the purple-grey *S. o.* 'Purpurescens' and will associate well with *Origanum* 'Aureum' and similar plants to form a low colourful tapestry of foliage, at the same time keeping down weeds; *Lamium maculatum* and the various forms of *Ajuga reptans* also associate well. Set 30 cm (1 ft) apart.

*** **Santolina.** The cotton lavenders make good ground cover if clipped over after flowering to keep them dense. They grow to 45 to 60 cm (18 in to 2 ft) and need conditions similar to those for rosemary and the sages—well drained soil and full sun. I do not care for the mustardy flower bobbles of some of the species so I recommend *S. neapolitana* 'Sulphurea' which has grey-green filigree foliage and pale primrose flower heads, or *S. virens* with bright green foliage and lemon-yellow flowers. Set 60 cm (2 ft) apart.

** **Saponaria ocymoides.** The old-fashioned double forms of the soapwort are worth growing in good border soil as they are vigorous enough to keep down weeds. Set 20 cm (8 in) apart.

*** **Sedum.** *Sedum maximum* in its variety *atropurpureum*, *S.* 'Autumn Joy', *Sedum spectabile* in the type and *S. s.* 'Brilliant', are efficient weed-suppressors, growing to a height of 45 cm (18 in). Plant as many varieties as possible for the varying tones of their thick, fleshy foliage which ranges from the fresh, pale green of the typical ice plant to the purple *atropurpureum*, the ruddy foliage tones of 'Autumn Joy' and the glaucous blue of 'Brilliant'. Each clump sprawls to give 0·1 sq m (1 sq ft) or more of effective cover. The sedums are easily increased by detaching some of the rooted outer stems in spring, and replanting in good soil. Set 30 cm (1 ft) apart.

*** **Senecio greyi.** One of the best ground-covering shrubs. Although potentially large and apt to sprawl if not cut back, it may be sheared over after flowering (or before if you do not like its sunny lemon 'daisies'), and will then remain a neat, wide hummock of about 90 cm (3 ft) or more. Set 90 cm (3 ft) apart.

*** **Stachys lanata.** Lamb's ears is one of my favourite plants and its woolly grey leaves make dense mats to keep down the weeds, provided the flowered stems are removed and the clumps are occasionally divided, in which process the old, worn-out centres are discarded and the outer pieces set to form new plantings. Evergrey, it will succeed in any freely draining soil in sun. Set 45 cm (18 in) apart.

** **Symphytum grandiflorum.** I used to think that this comfrey was one of the best of all ground covers, but for some years now it has been subject to rust and although it is evergreen and its growth is dense enough to keep down weeds, it looks untidy until the new leaves come to replace the ones that the rust has killed. It is still worth using in waste places or in large shrub plantings where its creamy crozier flowers will be appealing in early spring. Set 45 cm (18 in) apart.

*** **Trachystemon orientalis.** A coarse-leaved weed-suppressor, this plant should be limited to rough ground where the weed problem is desperate. It is attractive with large, hairy leaves and branches of pretty light blue flowers and grows to a height of 75 cm (2½ ft). Set 60 cm (2 ft) apart.

*** **Viburnum plicatum** 'Rowallane'. An exceptionally fine weed-suppressing shrub with a tired habit and dense leafage. In May and June the horizontal branches are a froth of large, white lacecap-hydrangea-type flowers with a spread of up to 0·5 sq m (6 sq ft). Upward-growing shoots should be removed to keep the plant to a low mound of 90 cm (3 ft) or so in height.

*** **Vinca minor.** Provided they are clipped over after flowering to keep them dense and free-blooming, the dwarf periwinkles are among the best weed-suppressing carpeters. Forms may be obtained with flowers of burgundy, pale and dark blue, or white. Some have variegated leaves and some double-flowered forms can sometimes be obtained. The variegated forms are less dense, however, than the others, but all are so pleasing that I would plant as many as possible. Rooting as they trail, each plant provides its own means of ready increase, and rooted stems can always be detached to create new plantings. Set 45 cm (18 in) apart.

*** **Viola cornuta.** This plant with its small pansy-type blooms in lilac, white or dark velvety purple, makes surprisingly good ground cover. Cut back hard in summer, the dense leafage will keep down weeds on rose beds or in the flower border, while the spring and autumn blooms set off the other occupants to great advantage. *V. cornuta* 'Alba' has the most rapid spread. Set 30 cm (1 ft) apart.

In addition to the plants listed, the various ferns and some of the more vigorous grasses may be used as weed-suppressing ground cover. In our garden we use the striped gardener's garters, *Phalaris arundinacea* 'Picta', to set off the purple-leafed berberis. It would also be most effective with the purple hazel-nut or with the dark-leafed burning bush (or smoke tree) *Cotinus coggygria purpureus* (rhus).

Various plants that naturalize themselves, seeding and increasing on their own account, are also to be encouraged, and care should be taken when weeding that they are not inadvertently eliminated. Among these I would encourage the various strains of foxglove, hellebore, hardy geranium, columbine, borage, honesty, annual candytuft, limnanthes (the annual poached-egg plant), and *Meconopsis cambrica* (the Welsh poppy). Some shrubs such as the prostrate cotoneasters and hardy fuchsia may also seed and the seedlings can be replanted where suitable.

TOP TEN GENERAL-PURPOSE WEED-SUPPRESSORS

Bergenia
Cotoneaster dammeri
Erica carnea 'Springwood'
Epimedium
Geranium (hardy species)
Hosta
Juniper (ground-covering types)
Senecio greyi
Viburnum plicatum 'Rowallane'
Vinca (periwinkle—dwarf forms)

BEST FOR WET GROUND

Astilbe
Ligularia 'Desdemona'
Lysichitum
Rodgersia

GROUND COVER FOR ROSE BEDS

Campanula portenschlagiana
  (*muralis*)
Dianthus Highland Hybrids
Saponaria ocymoides
Viola cornuta

'COMMUNE' PLANTS FOR SUNNY SPOTS

Cistus
Juniper
Phlomis fruticosa
Rosmarinus lavendulaceus
Ruta graveolens
Santolina
Salvia officinalis

BEST FOR POOR, DRY SOIL

Genista hispanica
Hedera (ivy)
Hypericum calycinum
Juniper
Pachysandra

BEST FOR DRY SHADE

Hedera (ivy)
Hydrangea petiolaris
Hypericum calycinum
Pachysandra

FOUR

The Right Plants in the Right Places

Weekend gardeners and those who through circumstances are forced to be away from their gardens for regular or irregular absences, are forced to depend on happy, trouble-free plants for their major effects. They have no opportunity to coddle invalids, to coerce lime-haters to thrive in borderline soils, or to watch over the miffy ones—however beautiful. For them the truism that 'handsome is as handsome does' is all important to their philosophy, so it is fortunate that there are many hearty, healthy plants which given the right conditions will flourish on little attention.

However 'trouble-free' a plant may be, it is dependent on being planted in a congenial place if it is to do its best. Even the easy, beautiful globe flower, the trollius of early spring, gives but a poor return in dry soil. Found in nature in damp meadows it needs moisture and good soil to fulfil its potential. Likewise the delightfully aromatic prostrate rosemary, *Rosmarinus lavendulaceus*, would quickly succumb to frost and winter damp if grown in the average rich, flat soil of the flower border. It needs sharp drainage and full sun to approximate to the Mediterranean sea-cliffs which are its natural home. The lovely *Monarda didyma*, the bergamot of gardens, is another case in point. Aromatic and herbal, by association one might expect that it would need the sharp drainage that the sages and marjoram love. On the contrary it must have a moist, rich soil if it is not to die out.

It is important when deciding on a site for a new plant to consider its needs. Those of many plants are given in this book and many more can be found in catalogues and encyclopaedias of gardening. If in doubt as to the natural habitat of any plant, be sure to look it up. Good money spent on buying a long-desired subject can be thrown away if one is not prepared to take the trouble to find out the kind of habitat it prefers.

Sometimes clues may be found in the foliage. Grey or glaucous leaves usually indicate a sun-lover, as does the presence of leaf-hairs. This blankety-type of foliage is designed to cut down the rate of transpiration (giving off water) through the leaves. Silky, hairy and suede-like coverings are nature's devices to regulate moisture loss. Sun-lovers coming from desert or semi-desert regions have thick, fleshy, water-retaining leaves, as do the sedums and some of the cacti.

Small-leafed shrubs generally come from open, windy conditions. The smallness of their leaf area is again intended to reduce the water loss by transpiration and also to avoid wind damage. In the genus *Rhododendron*, leaf types vary from the large-leafed giants of the rainy forest areas to the tiny-foliaged, dwarf, hummocky species that are found on the moorlands and mountains of Asia. Such small-leafed types from the sunny, windy uplands quickly suffer from fungus and become drawn and spindly if grown in sheltered woodland. On the other hand, the large-leafed rhododendrons would become tattered and drought-stricken if given the heath-like conditions that the small species enjoy.

To achieve success the weekend gardener has to go along with nature rather than trying to extend the limits imposed by the soil and climate of his garden.

If your garden is cold and windy, then it is essential to grow only those plants which will tolerate such conditions and even thrive in spite of them. It means choosing tough deciduous shrubs, or the hardiest evergreens—juniper, holly, and fir—to form a barrier to filter the wind's initial attack. The silvery-foliaged, semi-evergreen *Atriplex halimus* will do particularly well near the sea although in some winters it may be completely defoliated. Elsewhere elder, sycamore and other natives, periodically topped, can be mingled with gorse to keep out the wind.

In small gardens the outer barrier can best be supplied by a hedge of beech or hornbeam, according to soil. Beech will grow on sand, chalk, or gravelly, light soils, but for cold, wet ground hornbeam would be a wiser choice. Either may be mixed with holly to achieve a warmer-looking winter effect. If the beech is clipped in August it will retain most of its dead, brown leaves during the winter and these will combine attractively with the green of the holly.

Alternatively, a mixed hedge, such as often seen on farmland, could combine hawthorn, sycamore, elder, holly, hornbeam or beech to form an impenetrable and attractive barrier. In our own garden my husband and I planted a mixed hedge of evergreen and deciduous flowering shrubs along the western boundary.

With our garden in Wales, being a quarter of a mile from the sea and exposed to the south-westerly gales, it was necessary to establish a tall wind-break 2·5 m (8 ft) in height to filter the wind sufficiently to enable us to grow our favourite camellias, tree paeonies, and small rhododendrons without damage. Our mixed hedge was composed of forsythia, weigela, laburnum (annually topped), *Cotoneaster lacteus* and *C. simonsii*, *Hebe salicifolia*, ribes (flowering currant), philadelphus and olearia, with roses 'Emily Grey' and 'Albertine'.

Honeysuckle may be encouraged in a mixed hedge so long as it is not allowed completely to take control. Its fragrance and blossom add a great deal to the summer charm of the hedge and if both the early and late Dutch types are planted, a long season of blossom is achieved. The evergreen *Lonicera japonica halliana*, however, should never be used in such a situation. It is far too invasive and will eventually choke everything else.

Where only a fence exists, *Hedera* 'Hibernica' (the Irish ivy) may be grown up open mesh wire, quickly to form an effective wind-break. Hurdles and interlap fencing are not to be despised where shelter must be established as a matter of urgent priority, although I would always plant a hedge of mixed shrubs on the inside against the day when the hurdles eventually begin to disintegrate.

For those who do not object to concrete, a screen of open-work blocks will give more permanent protection, and may be disguised by wall shrubs on the inside.

Once shelter has been achieved, some of the choicer flowering shrubs and plants can be established. It is important for the absent gardener to remember that he may well not be on hand when any additional protection may be needed, so he should always allow himself to be guided by the criterion of hardiness. Staking, too, is a complication that he can well forgo. In really windy gardens even the most unlikely plants such as the tree paeonies, border irises, and Darwin tulips can need staking. To play safe one should choose only those plants which rely entirely on their own support. This means depending on sturdy plants such as lupins, the dwarfer erigerons with their selection of pink and mauve 'daisies'; aconitum (monkshood); *Coreopsis verticillata*; the dwarf valerian; and *Stachys macrantha* 'Superba', and *S. lanata*. If you want to plant a solidago, golden rod, you should choose the dwarf 'Queenie' which is only 25 cm (10 in) high.

If you want irises, choose the dwarf bearded varieties, or the taller *I. sibirica* cultivars if you have a spot with a damp, rich soil where they can be planted; or opt out and settle for the iris-like member of the same family, the yellow-flowered *Sisyrinchium striatum* which grows to no more than 45 cm (18 in), with whippy, flower-laden stems.

Other hardy plants which will succeed include *Senecio doronicum* with
bright orange 'daisies' on 30 cm (12 in) stems; the dwarf *Saponaria
ocymoides*; nepeta, catmint; pulmonaria; the various Asiatic primula
species (if your soil is moist); *Polemonium caeruleum*, Jacob's ladder;
physostegia, the obedient plant; oriental poppy; *Hypericum olympicum*;
hemerocallis, day lily; *Helenium* 'Wyndley' which grows to only 60 cm
(2 ft); hardy geraniums; *Doronicum plantagineum* 'Miss Mason' (the
dwarfest variety); *Chrysanthemum arcticum* growing to 30 cm (12 in),
with pink 'daisies'; centaurea, cornflower; *Campanula portenschlagiana*
(syn. *C. muralis*) and the dwarf *C. lactiflora* 'Pouffe'; *Caltha palustris*
'Flore Pleno' (a double kingcup for a moist patch); dwarf Michaelmas
daisies, and Japanese anemones.

Some trees for cold, exposed places are *Acer pseudoplatanus*, sycamore; *Crataegus monogyna*, common hawthorn; laburnum; *Populus*
'Robusta' and *P.* 'Serotina', poplar; *Sorbus aria*, whitebeam; *S.
aucuparia*, mountain ash, and *Tilia cordata*, lime.

Some shrubs for cold, exposed places include calluna, ling; *Cornus
alba* and its variegated forms; *Cotinus coggygria purpureus*, burning bush
or smoke tree; *Euonymus fortunei* and *E. japonica*; *Gaultheria shallon*;
Hipphopae rhamnoides, sea buckthorn; *Hydrangea paniculata* 'Grandiflora';
Kalmia angustifolia and *K. latifolia* (for acid soil); *Kerria japonica*; *Mahonia
aquifolium*; pernettya; philadelphus, mock orange; rhododendron hardy
hybrids and *R. yakushimanum*; salix, willow; spiraea; tamarix, and
Viburnum opulus.

Conifers for cold exposed places include *Chamaecyparis nootkatensis*;
C. obtusa; *C. pisifera*; *Cryptomeria japonica*; Japanese cedar; ginkgo;
junipers; larch; *Picea abies*, the Christmas tree; *Pinus nigra*, Austrian
pine; *P. pinaster*, maritime pine; taxus, yew, and thuja.

Chalk and lime present problems in that lime-sensitive plants sicken and
die on such soils. Rhododendrons, camellias, some magnolias, and
most Japanese and North American shrubs will not thrive. On the
other hand, lime-loving genera will do exceptionally well.

A mechanical difficulty occurs on chalk soils where a hard-pan often
underlies a poor, shallow top-soil by only a few inches. This must
be broken up into rubble with a pick-axe before other than the shal-
lowest-rooted herbaceous plants can succeed. Once this is done, the
rubble will prove to have valuable moisture-holding properties.

Most chalk and limestone soils are hungry and however much one
feeds them a great deal of the nutriment will always leach away. When
mulching it is important to use coarse material containing as much
nourishment as possible. Seaweed, coarse peat, hop-manure, shoddy,

horse-manure and deep-litter from poultry farms are all helpful, while it goes almost without saying that one should compost all the garden rubbish one possibly can. Weekend gardeners may find the newer 'Rotovator' bins a help in enabling them easily and tidily to make a good compost.

For a beautiful and self-maintaining garden of chalk, the absent gardener should take care (1) always to break up the hard-pan sub-soil before planting; (2) always to mulch with material as coarse as possible; (3) to choose only those plants which are known to do well in alkaline soils and which have the necessary coarse root system.

This last is not as difficult as it sounds. Many genera excel on chalk, including the beautiful and fragrant viburnums, the lilacs, philadelphus, genista, wisteria, clematis, dianthus, and chaenomeles (cydonia). Many others are accommodating, amongst them the forsythias, some of the berberis—in particular *B. darwinii* and *B. × stenophylla*—osmanthus and × osmarea; *Erinacea anthyllis* (*pungens*), the pretty hedgehog broom; ceanothus; staphylea, bladder nut; prunus; kolkwitzia; deutzia; buddleia; hebe; hypericum; senecio; potentilla; ceratostigma; caryopteris; indigofera; romneya, the beautiful shrubby Californian poppy; cotoneaster; stranvaesia; *Euonymus alatus* and *E. yedoensis*, spindleberry; ilex, holly; *Skimmia japonica*; pyracantha; mahonia; chimonanthus, winter sweet; *Erica mediterranea* and *E. stricta*; salix, willow; stachyurus; corylus, hazel; and corylopsis. These will give a year-round coverage of interest and flowers.

Rose-lovers will find that it is the coarser-growing hybrid tea roses and floribundas which succeed best in chalky soil, just as they do in clay. Here the rule is always to go for vigour when making one's selection. It has sometimes been said that the Japanese *Rosa rugosa*, perpetual-flowering shrub roses, will not grow on chalk, but luckily this statement is not at all borne out by fact. Many Japanese shrubs will not tolerate alkaline conditions, but *R. rugosa* is a notable exception. Completely disease-free and seldom subject to aphis, the varieties of this species make dense, mounded bushes with tough foliage and pleasing single or semi-double blooms of the old-fashioned type. Most are delightfully fragrant and carry large, decorative, tomato-shaped hips.

The true species and its cultivars have single flowers in pink, crimson or white and fruit particularly well in autumn after flowering the summer through. Some of the hybrids, however, tend to become leggy, especially 'Conrad F. Meyer', and the otherwise extremely desirable pink 'Sarah van Fleet'. The 'Grootendorst' varieties which have small flowers with fringed petals carried in clusters like bunches of pink or red carnations are pleasing but rather gaunt. The soft pink 'Fimbriata' is the best fringed type. Hybrids which, if grown in the open, make dense mounded bushes, 90 cm (3 ft) high and wide, which keep down their own weeds, are the semi-double, white 'Blanc double de Coubert', semi-double pink 'Belle de Poitevine', the crimson 'Roseraie de l'Hay', and the beautiful, soft pink 'Frau Dagmar Hastrupp'. This last may be a cultivar of the species. 'Schneezwerg', too, is pretty, with smaller but very brightly coloured hips often carried along with the autumn burst of bloom.

It must be emphasized that these Japanese rugosa roses, although continuous in flower, have the aspect of shrub or old-fashioned roses and do not perhaps fulfil the average gardener's idea of a 'rose' as typified by the hybrid teas. They are, however, the answer to many a weekend gardener's prayer. They are totally immune to mildew and black spot; moreover, they shed their spent blooms at once, so there is no returning on a Friday night to be confronted by the sorry mess of brown and badly dying blooms, as so often happens with the more conventional roses.

Whether one gardens on chalk, lime, acid heathland, poor sandy soil, good loam or even clay, the rugosa roses make happy and hearty bushes. They are the only truly trouble-free roses in my experience.

With sandy or stony soils, the weekend gardener shares some of the difficulties of those who garden on chalk or lime. Their soils are hungry and so need adequate mulching with humus-laden material. Stones, in themselves, present no problem. Contrary to an often-held belief, they are beneficial rather than a hindrance—unless one wishes to cultivate straight-rooted carrots or parsnips for show. Stones assist drainage and aeration, and a scattering of stone on the surface acts as a mulch in helping to conserve moisture. There are some problems, however, with stony soils, due to lack of tilth and nourishment, and to the fact that they offer only a poor root-hold.

Plants grown in sandy or stony soils are apt to suffer badly from drought. This can best be helped by mulching, and by leaving a saucer-shaped depression around the stem of trees and shrubs when planting. In such soils water will never lie long enough to cause basal rot, and the saucer will collect water when it falls, thus ensuring that plenty of moisture gets to the actual root area. One can help further by incorporating plenty of thoroughly soaked, wet peat when planting. Soaked newspapers also help if used to line the planting hole or trench.

Wind-rock is an occurrence that can cause a great deal of nuisance to the absent gardener who is not on hand to carry out emergency staking or to replace broken ties during a gale. To help offset this trouble one can place a large stone or boulder over the roots of any very exposed subjects. I usually place the first spadeful of soil over the roots when planting and then put a boulder to windward of the main stem, anchoring the roots before filling in with the remainder of the soil. This particularly necessary when planting brooms, ceanothus or any half-standard or standard trees which present considerable sail area. In poor soils and on windy sites it is usually safer to plant a bush-type tree in preference to a standard or half-standard. If the growth forks low down, there is less liability for the wind to snatch the top growth of the tree, and either snap the stem or wrench it out of the ground.

Seaside gardens are so often the province of weekend gardeners that Chapter Seven is devoted entirely to this subject.

Streams and pools are delightful garden assets but they often present a problem in that the damp ground seems to encourage weed growth. This can best be offset by using self-gardening ground cover of the type recommended in the previous chapter. Where a plot is incurably marshy it is best to limit one's plantings to subjects known to succeed in such a site.

Some trees for damp sites include *Betula nigra, B. pendula* and *B. pubescens,* birch; *Crataegus oxycantha,* ornamental thorn; *Magnolia virginiana*; populus, poplar; salix, willow, and *Sorbus aucuparia,* mountain ash.

Of the conifers only *Metasequoia glyptostroboides,* dawn redwood; *Taxodium distichum,* swamp cypress; and *Picea sitchensis* can be recommended.

Amongst shrubs for damp sites are clethra, sweet pepper; *Cornus alba* and cultivars, common dogwoods including red-stemmed and variegated types; *Gaultheria shallon; Hippophae rhamnoides,* sea buckthorn; *Ilex verticillata,* black alder; *Myrica gale,* bog myrtle; *Neillia thibetica (longiracemosa)*; salix, dwarf willow species; sambucus, elder; *Spiraea × vanhouttei* and *S. veitchii; Symphoricarpus albus,* snowberry; vaccinium (especially on acid soil), and *Viburnum opulus* and cultivars. Bamboos such as the *Arundinaria* species are also suitable but care must be taken not to plant too rampant sorts.

Add to these such herbaceous plants as the giant rheums, the rodgersias, ligularias, *Iris pseudacorus* and *I. sibirica,* the many colourful varieties of astilbe, the bog primulas such as the tall Himalayan cowslip, the Asiatic candelabra primulas and the small, very bright, early-spring-blooming *Primula rosea*, along with caltha (marsh marigolds) and the lysichitums, and the possibility of making a problem patch of moist ground into an interesting and reasonably weed-free piece of garden becomes reality even for the absent gardener.

Clay soils can be improved by the addition of coarse humus and by using proprietary treatments such as the reliable *Acta-Bacta* and *Clay Cure*, together with the burning of recalcitrant lumps of clay on a slow bonfire before reincorporating them in the soil. Wood ash is also particularly helpful. All this attention takes time and trouble but the weekend gardener may well devote what leisure he can spare to it. Meanwhile it helps to plant only coarse-rooted herbaceous plants. the more vigorous roses, and such trees and shrubs as are contained in the following lists.

Some trees for clay soils are acer, maple, all species; aesculus, horse chestnut; betula, birch; carpinus, hornbeam; crataegus, thorn; eucalyptus (except in cold areas); ilex, holly; laburnum; malus, crab apple; populus, poplar; prunus, cherry, apricot and plum; quercus, oak; salix, willow; sorbus, and tilia, lime.

Most conifers, including metasequoia, thujopsis, ginkgo and tsuga, will succeed but not the true *Cupressus* species.

For shrubs that will do well in clay choose from abelia; aralia; aucuba; berberis; chaenomeles; *Choisya ternata*, Mexican orange blossom; cornus; corylus, hazel; cotinus, cotoneaster; cytisus, broom; deutzia; escallonia; forsythia; genista; hamamelis, witch hazel; hardy hibiscus; hypericum; lonicera; mahonia; magnolia; osmanthus and × *Osmare*; (the latter for cold areas); philadelphus, mock orange; potentilla; pyracantha; rhododendron (provided the clay is not alkaline); ribes, flowering currant; roses (the more vigorous types do best); *Senecio greyi*; skimmia; spiraea; *Symphoricarpus albus*; viburnum and weigela.

Heathland and dry acid soils have their limitations but attractive and easily maintained gardens can be made provided one follows nature in deciding on the type of planting. Beds of erica (heath) and calluna (ling), dwarf and large rhododendrons (including azaleas) could predominate with birches, pernettya (berried ground cover) and berberis, combined with some of the following trees and shrubs.

Some trees for heathland are *Acer negundo*; ailanthus, tree of heaven; castanea, chestnut; *Cercis siliquastrum*, Judas tree; ilex; *Populus alba* and *P. tremula*; robinia and *Ulmus pumila*, dwarf elm.

Shrubs and trees for heathland include cistus; *Colutea arborescens*, bladder senna; cotoneaster; elaeagnus especially the variegated *E.*

pungens 'Maculata' and *E.* × *ebbingei*; genista; hibiscus (hardy); indigo-fera; *Kerria japonica*; lonicera; *Rosa pimpinellifolia*, burnet rose; *Salix caprea*, goat willow; tamarix and ulex, gorse. All junipers, pines and *Cupressus glabra* varieties will also succeed.

For this type of garden some of the dwarf rhododendron species and hybrids make excellent ground cover for the absent gardener's purpose, as when they are established the area gardened by them will need weeding only once or twice a year. Dwarfs such as *R. scintillans*, *R. chryseum*, *R. microleucum*, *R. hanceanum* 'Nanum', *R. charitopes* and *R. campylogynum myrtilloides* make dense hummocks of foliage in an open, airy place. They may be helped by the addition of some of the larger-growing, but still miniature-flowered, hybrids such as 'Pink Drift', 'Blue Diamond', 'Augfast' and 'Sapphire'. A little larger in leaf and with sizeable, waxy hanging bells of flower is the scarlet-crimson 'Humming Bird', which gives particularly dense leaf-cover, as will its parent, *R. williamsianum*, with similar mounded growth, rounded leaf-shape, and hanging pink bells. *R. williamsianum*, in particular, stands clipping well.

Heavy shade can be a problem so a list of suitable shrubs and trees may be helpful. My recommendations are *Arctostaphylos uva-ursi*, bearberry; *Aucuba japonica*; *Camellia japonica* and *C.* × *williamsii*; the creeping dogwood, *Cornus canadensis*; *Daphne laureola* and *D. pontica*; elaeagnus; *Euonymus fortunei*; × *Fatshedera lizei*; *Fatsia japonica*; gaultheria; *Hedera helix* 'Aborescens'; *Hypericum androsaemum* and *H. calycinum*; *Ilex aquifolium*, holly; *Lonicera pileata* (to give ground cover); *Mahonia aquifolium*; pachysandra; *Prunus laurocerasus*, common or cherry laurel, and *P. lusitanica*, Portugal laurel; *Rhododendron ponticum* and hardy hybrids (these may not flower well); hydrangea (if ground is not too dry); *Ribes alpinum*; *Rubus spectabilis* and *R. tricolor*; ruscus; *Sarcococca humilis* (to give ground cover); skimmia; *Viburnum davidii* (turquoise berries, to obtain which plants of both sexes are needed); vinca; *Juniperus media* 'Pfitzeriana'. Podocarpus and taxus will also grow in shade.

Bulbous plants such as lily of the valley, erythronium (dog's tooth violet), daffodils and some lilies will thrive in shade if the ground is not too dry and provided there is plenty of humus in the soil. To these may be added Solomon's seal, many primulas, the 'Mermaid' rose and *Rosa* 'Mme Alfred Carrière', astilbes if the soil is rich, also hostas, hellebores, hardy geraniums and ferns.

Some further suggestions for plants to choose for various sites and soil conditions are made in Chapter Six under 'Planting According to Soil and Aspect', p. 105.

FIVE

Long-Season Performers

Those who see their gardens only at weekends or holiday periods often miss the brief flowering of some of their plants. This is particularly true of some shrubs such as the amalanchiers (snowy mespilus), the single-flowered cherries-apart from the autumn-blooming and earliest spring varieties—and the single lilacs. These may come to full glory on the Monday or Tuesday, then be blown to pieces by a mid-week gale, and by the time the garden-owner returns on Friday night show only a few fading blossoms and a carpet of shattered blooms.

The absent gardener's priority in plant selection must be the length of time each tree, shrub, bulb or herbaceous plant remains at its best. In the case of shrubs and trees the season of interest may be extended by fruit or foliage beauty. The variegated leaves of the *Weigela florida* 'Variegata' add colour and interest from April until November but the beauty of its pink foxglove-like flowers lasts little more than a fortnight at best.

Some shrubs and trees will be grown mainly for their foliage. Among these are the *Elaeagnus* species and hybrids of which the silver-leafed *E.* × *ebbingei* and the slightly tender *E. macrophylla* have a bonus of tiny white, scented fuchsia-like flowers in autumn, once the plants have become well established. The purple-foliaged *Berberis thunbergii atropurpurea* is not outstanding in flower, yet it is worth a place in any garden for its leaf colour.

It should be noted here that most colourful foliage shrubs need the association of others with different foliage tones if they are to achieve their full effect in the garden. A scheme composed of the tallish golden conifer *Chamaecyparis lawsoniana* 'Stewartii', contrasted with the rounded shape and rich dark purple-red foliage of *Cotinus coggygria* 'Royal Purple', with the low-spreading, blue-grey *Juniperus horizontalis* 'Bar Harbor' nearby, will have much greater impact than would the same subjects scattered in isolation throughout the garden.

Berries, too, are important, prolonging the attraction of a tree or shrub and giving it a second season of colour and interest. Some of the pyrancanthas, cotoneasters and sorbus are effective in flower, their heavily laden branches covered in a froth of creamy or white blossom in May, but their second and even more important spell of beauty comes in autumn when their scarlet, yellow, white or orange berries provide a note of warmth in the increasingly chilly scene.

Many of the honeysuckles—plants which one tends to think of only in connection with their scented flowers—have showy, scarlet-to-crimson berries at the summer's end.

SHRUBS AND TREES WITH THE LONGEST SEASON OF INTEREST

Abelia. Although many textbooks say that the abelias are tender, given a well-drained soil in full sunshine they will withstand the hardest winters in many gardens. The small-growing *A. schumannii*, 90 cm (3 ft) high and wide, has the longest season of bloom with an abundant and continuous display of its lilac-pink funnel-shaped flowers in late summer.

Abutilon (warm gardens only). The handsome *A. vitifolium* 'Album' deserves a protected site against a sunny wall. It grows to 1·5 m (5 ft) in height with a 90 cm (3 ft) spread. The white saucer-shaped flowers are carried throughout the season against downy, grey, vine-shaped leaves. Gardeners who dislike white flowers—and I know there are some—might prefer the large, mauve-blossomed *A. v.* 'Veronica Tennant'.

Acer (foliage). Interest from spring to late autumn can be obtained from the beautiful Japanese maples—*A. palmatum* cultivars. All need a neutral-to-acid soil. The best value plant in this group is *A. p.* 'Atropurpureum', the leaf colour of which lasts throughout the season. Also good are those of the Dissectum group with their lacy, filigree foliage. They are particularly good garden value as their dense, umbrella shape effectively keeps down weeds beneath their domes. Unfortunately the yellow form, 'Dissectum Flavescens', changes to green during the summer. *A. palmatum* 'Aureum', however, retains its golden-yellow leaf colour. All the maples assume fine autumn tints. Slow growing, they should nevertheless be allotted an area nearly 2 m (6 ft) square, ground-cover plants being used to fill in during the years before they reach maturity.

Aralia (foliage). Only the variegated forms of this genus are worth space in the average garden. 'Aureovariegata', as might be expected, has yellow-splashed leaves in spring, while 'Variegata' itself is marked with creamy white. In summer, however, both become variegated with silver white. The huge, doubly pinnate leaves are very striking although usually borne aloft on rather a leggy plant. Allow a space nearly 2 m (6 ft) square.

Arbutus (flower and berry). For heathland gardens and most shrub belts, the lime-tolerant *A. unedo*, the strawberry tree, is a reliable wind-hardy shrub. It is evergreen and its lily-of-the-valley-like flowers are followed by green-and-crimson, strawberry-like fruits produced in the late autumn. It is a decorative shrub to cut for taking back to town, at a time when flowers are expensive and scarce. It grows to a height of 1·7 m (6 ft) with a 1·2 m (4 ft) spread.

Berberis (foliage—some, flower and berry, giving a long season of interest). Easy and accommodating, this genus contains a particularly useful coloured foliage variety in the moderate-growing *B. thunbergii atropurpurea*. The vivid-flowered evergreen *B. linearifolia* 'Orange King' is worth planting for the long-lasting quality of its drooping bunches of bloom, while the best in berry is the tall *B. jamesiana*, which bears lemon-yellow flowers in spring and has good autumn colour, followed by prolific crops of coral-red berries.

Most members of the genus, however, are so spiny that working among them becomes purgatory, and there is a strong case for mulching heavily around them with pine bark to suppress all weeds. Sizes range from the modest 90 by 90 cm (3 by 3 ft) *B. thunbergii* to the 2·5 by 1·5 m (8 by 5 ft) seldom seen but brilliant-berried *B. vulgaris*. *B. darwinii*, with its large clusters of orange-yellow blossom, followed by purple berries, may even grow to 3 m (10 ft) and, though extremely spiny, is a very welcome early spring flowerer.

Buddleia. *B. alternifolia* is the only hardy member of the family that I consider worth growing. The blossoms of the *B. davidii* varieties, and even of the delectable *B. fallowiana*, too quickly turn brown. *B. alternifolia*, however, has an attractive weeping habit to add to the prettiness of its sweetly scented, lilac-mauve flower spikes in June.

Calluna vulgaris, ling. This has many modern cultivars with coloured foliage, that make attractive plantings for acid soil, with single or double flowers in shades of pink, purple or white; the foliage colours range from bright yellow to orange, often tipped when young with pink. A study of a good catalogue will enable you to make your own choice. 'Silver Queen', 'Gold Haze', 'Orange Queen', 'Robert Chapman' and 'Blazeaway' are among the best, giving double value in foliage and flower. This genus will grow to 45 cm (18 in) with a spread of 75 cm (2 ft 6 in).

Camellia (evergreen with handsome foliage). With long-lasting flowers, except in frosty areas, this plant is lime-sensitive. For the garden with reasonably good frost protection, for planting against a north- or west-facing wall or fence, or beneath a canopy of deciduous tree branches, there is no better spring-blooming shrub than the camellia. Gardeners who are at home all the time and can cosset their camellias to persuade them to grow in tubs or raised beds, can succeed even in limy soils; but for the weekend gardener this is too great a risk. The best varieties for planting in acid soil are *C.* × *williamsii* 'Donation', luscious doublepink (a real bonus with the *williamsii* hybrids is that they drop their dead flowers); *C. japonica* 'Adolphe Audusson', a magnificent semi-double red; and the pale-pink informal *C. j.* 'Magnoliaeflora'. These three will give enough variety for the average gardener. White varieties quickly turn brown with bad weather and are not worth outdoor planting unless one is on hand to shelter the blooms. Allow a space nearly 2 m (6 ft) square.

Caryopteris clandonensis (valuable for late summer). Beloved for its cloud of bright, soft blue flowers in August and September, the caryopteris is good garden value, but needs sharp drainage and sun. Its aromatic foliage and low, mounded habit make it a potential member for a 'commune' planting of sun-loving shrubs. It associates particularly well with the coppery-yellow flowers of *Potentilla fruticosa* 'Tangerine' or 'Day Dawn'. It will tolerate chalk. Allow a space 90 by 120 cm (3 by 4 ft).

Ceanothus (deciduous or evergreen—not for cold areas). The best value shrub in this genus is the evergreen long-blooming *C.* 'Burkwoodii' which carries a sequence of its rich blue thimbles throughout summer and autumn. In some areas it needs a warm wall, but in the south and west it is hardy in the open in most gardens. Colder places can enjoy a show of softer blue in late summer by planting the deciduous *C.* 'Gloire de Versailles'. This should be pruned back each spring. Allow a space nearly 2 m (6 ft) square.

Where a maquis-type 'commune' of sun-lovers is envisaged to cover a well-drained sunny bank, *C. prostratus*, the squaw carpet of California, could be planted for its sheets of blue in spring. Its dense foliage also makes useful ground cover. The ceanothus are subject to wind-rock, so in exposed areas a boulder to windward of the stem should be placed over the roots at planting time.

Cercis siliquastrum, Judas tree. In its new cultivar 'Bodnant', this spreading small tree is so outstanding in its early summer flower that it should be planted wherever possible. The glory of its deep rose-purple pea flowers seldom lasts for more than a fortnight, but its sea-green, heart-shaped foliage is always attractive and colours well in autumn. In cold places the Judas tree can be trained against a wall; elsewhere it needs a sheltered place in full sun. Allow a space 2·5 by 3·7 m (8 by 12 ft).

Chaenomeles (valuable for early blossom). Well-known for the showy scarlet of its large, bowl-shaped flowers, *C.* × *superba* 'Knap Hill Scarlet' is one of the very best of the genus. Also good, and very early to bloom, is the semi-double, pale terracotta *C. speciosa* 'Phyllis Moore'. It is worth planting the different varieties in various aspects to prolong their flowering season. Against a warm wall, 'Phyllis Moore' will often come into bloom in January. Varieties in white and apple-blossom will be found in any comprehensive catalogue. On chalk and limestone, the chaenomeles may be widely planted to replace the dwarf rhododendrons and azaleas which would not grow there. The only nuisance is that they need to be pinched back in June when their soft stems are extending. Failing this, they should be cut back with the secateurs later in summer. When grown in the open ground, care must be taken to keep the centre of the bush open. It will occupy a space 120 by 90 cm (4 by 3 ft).

Chimonanthus, winter sweet. Where winter blossom is valued to take back to town after the weekend, the winter sweet is worth growing on limy soils where the superior witch hazel would not thrive. It should be given a sunny wall, and allowed a space 150 by 90 cm (5 by 3 ft).

Choisya ternata, Mexican orange blossom (not for cold gardens). Attractive in foliage and with fragrant white blossom in late spring and early summer, many people rate this medium-sized glossy-leafed shrub highly. It will grow in sun or shade, occupying a space 90 by 150 cm (3 by 5 ft).

Cistus (sun—not for cold gardens). This attractive genus has been covered fairly extensively in Chapter Three, but I would like to add here the taller and rather more gaunt *C.* × *cyprius*, which is reasonably hardy in most places and bears clusters of large, saucer-shaped blooms with a showy crimson basal blotch. For warm areas, the more tender rosy-pink *C.* × *purpureus* with a chocolate basal blotch is also a 'must'. Although each blossom lasts only a day, the bushes are in flower over a long period and usually bloom again in autumn. Allow a space 1½ by 1½ m (5 by 5 ft).

Clematis. Although strictly a climber, the clematis can be used to ramble through shrubs, thereby providing a longer season of flowering. In our garden we have the reliable old variety *C.* 'Nelly Moser', with large, pale-pink blooms striped with rose, climbing through the winter-blooming *Viburnum farreri* (*fragrans*). *Clematis* 'Jackmanni Superba' rambles through the rose 'Golden Showers', its deep purple-blue flowers contrasting well with those of the rose, and the dark-blue *C.* 'President', with its lighter pink bar, grows through the later-flowering, pale-blush-flowered *Fuchsia magellanica* 'Alba'.

Rhododendrons, corylopsis, weigela, all form suitable hosts. The charming, early-flowering *Clematis macropetala* will climb happily through the hummocky summer- and autumn-flowering hebes such as 'Blue Gem' and 'Autumn Queen'. Most hybrid clematis are suitable to grow through shrubs in this way and seldom need pruning unless it should become necessary to cut out tangled growth. The May-blooming pink and white *C. montana* and the autumn-flowering *C. tangutica* and *C. orientalis* are really too vigorous for this treatment although we grow the orange-peel clematis, *tangutica*, over a hedge.

C. montana 'Tetrarose' with its large soft pink blooms and bronzy foliage is particularly effective if grown through the branches of a large tree and allowed to shower downwards.

Cornus. Two types of dogwood are worth the attention of the week-end gardener. The first, *C. alba* 'Elegantissima', is valuable for its variegated silvery-green leaves edged with white, and for the reddish tints of its bare winter stems. Pollarding encourages a prolific growth of young stems and at the same time keeps the bush within bounds (2·5 by 2·5 m (8 by 8 ft)). The other type, as represented by *C. florida* and *C. nuttallii*, are grown for the beauty of their 'flowers'. These need a deep, non-chalky soil. *C. kousa*, not recommended for poor, chalky soil, has two seasons of beauty—in June when the large, long-lasting bracted flower-heads cover the large bushes with showy white stars, and in autumn when the foliage turns to bronze and crimson. A form of this species from China—*C. k. chinensis*—is said to grow on chalk. *C. florida*, likewise, depends for its flower display on large, long-lasting bracts. Its main season is in May, but it needs a hotter, sunnier place in order to flower well than does *kousa*, which succeeded well with us in Wales. In the south of England, *florida* does well, and there are several American cultivars, obtainable from Hilliers, which have pink to rose flower bracts. Of these 'Apple Blossom' is the palest, while 'Cherokee Chief' is a deep rose-red. 'Tricolor' has leaves that are attractively variegated with a creamy-white margin flushed with rose and they turn to bronzy purple in the autumn. This is a superb foliage shrub and may reach 4·5 m (15 ft) in height. All the well-known culti-vars colour well in autumn.

In the course of time some forms of *C. kousa* become large trees, as does the third of the 'flowering' species, *C. nuttallii*, with its large, showy, white-bracted 'flowers'. Its foliage turns yellow in autumn.

For mild areas only, *C. capitata* is the most beautiful species of the genus, forming a small shapely tree and carrying sulphur-yellow bracted flower-heads in June and July, followed in October by large strawberry-like fruits. *C. kousa* too carries similar 'strawberry' fruits though these are less showy than those of *capitata*.

Corylopsis (early spring flowers). This genus is useful to replace the spring effect of forsythia in gardens where the blossom of the latter is spoiled by the birds. The corylopsis is of more refined appearance than the forsythia, with its pretty cowslip-yellow blossoms borne before the leaves appear on the hazel-type bush. With the exception of *C. pauci-flora*, which will not grow on chalk, all are extremely accommodating as to soil. They will, however, make better growth and flower best in a sunny place in rich loam. *C. willmottiae* is, in my opinion, the best species for the average gardener to grow, carrying long, racemes of flowers, and making a medium-sized-to-quite-large shrub. There is a form 'Spring Purple', the young growth of which is an attractive plum-purple colour. Allow a space 2·5 by 1·7 m (8 by 6 ft).

Corylus maxima 'Purpurea' (foliage). A first-class, purple-leafed shrub, this is suitable for most soils and exposures. It is dual-purpose as it bears quantities of edible nuts. The only other hazel worth general cultivation is the attractively twisted *C. avellana* 'Contorta' which is at its most beautiful when in catkin in spring. Allow a space 2·7 m (8 ft) square.

Cotinus coggygria. In its 'Royal Purple' form the smoke tree is a fine foliage shrub with pleasing mounded habit and rounded wine-purple leaves which redden towards autumn. It is fairly slow in growth and eventually makes a shrub of from 1¼ to 2 m (4 to 6 ft), but if hard pruned in spring it can be kept more compact and will also yield better leaf-colour. The pinkish-fawn-coloured, smoke-like inflorescences are produced on mature shrubs in June and July. As far as colour is concerned, it is most effective if planted near a blue-flowered shrub such as the deciduous *Ceanothus* 'Gloire de Versailles'. It may also be placed in conjunction with a columnar blue conifer or one of spreading low growth such as *Juniperus horizontalis* 'Bar Harbor'.

Cotoneaster. Of this genus the most worthwhile from the absent gardener's viewpoint are those prostrate species which act as ground cover, adding the virtue of usefulness to the beauty of their berries in autumn. Foremost are *C. conspicuus* 'Decorus' and 'Highlight' which are extremely free-fruiting, form dense mounds of growth, and are useful to cover banks or to place in front of taller shrubs. 'Highlight' bears orange-red fruits which are especially showy. *C. dammeri* is a completely prostrate species, excellent for ground cover, with a complexity of dense shoots that are covered in autumn with sealing-wax-red berries. Both *dammeri* and *conscpicuus* are evergreen. Both will in time cover several square metres of ground. Of the taller cotoneasters the best, to my mind, is 'Hybridus Pendulus' when grown on a stem to make an attractively weeping small tree. It, too, is extremely free in berry and is evergreen.

Crataegus oxycantha, common hawthorn. The genus is not worth growing in rich soil because this leads to an excess of growth over flower. In stony, poor soil, or on dry banks it reaches a fine peak of flowering and remains in beauty for two to three weeks at the end of May and into June. As with most genera, the double-flowered forms last longest in flower. My own favourites are 'Paul's Scarlet' and the old 'Rosea Flore Pleno'. The double white, called simply 'Plena', is also worth growing and very showy when in flower. Allow a space 3·7 m (12 ft) square.

Crinodendron hookerianum, the Chilean lantern bush (warm areas). This shrub is hardy in the south and west and we found it quite hardy to within five miles of the sea in North Wales. It is a valuable evergreen as its large rosy-crimson lanterns last well and give it the appearance of a giant fuchsia when in flower. As a precaution it should be given a site with good air drainage and is worth wall protection in areas where its hardiness might be in doubt. Apart from this it needs a chalk-free soil and partial shade, or at least a deep, fairly moist soil. It is one of the best seaside subjects so long as it can be planted out of reach of salt spray. Upright growing, it will in time occupy a 2 by 1 m (8 by 5 ft) space.

Cytisus. The earlier-flowering brooms have the longest flowering period. Unfortunately few of the hybrids succeed on chalk, so gardeners with chalky soil should plant the more easily accommodated *Genista* species instead. *Cytisus × praecox*, the sulphur-flowered spring broom, is one of the best of the genus. It has various cultivars, two of the best being 'Albus' (white) and 'Allgold' (a deep yellow). They last in flower for three weeks or more, and will occupy a space 1·7 by 2·5 m (6 by 8 ft). In our own garden we find *C. multiflorus* worthwhile too. Slightly later to flower, this white broom from Portugal reaches 2 m (6ft or more) in height with a comparable spread. It associates well with the rosy-lilac tree heath, *Erica australis*, though unfortunately the latter may be too tender for some cold gardens. Both it and the broom need acid or neutral well-drained soil.

A later-blooming species, *Cytisus nigricans*, lasts for a long time in flower, its long, terminal racemes of yellow being produced continuously throughout the late summer. This species associates well with blue hydrangeas, soft blue *Caryopteris × clandonensis* and the powder blue of deciduous *Ceanothus* 'Gloire de Versailles'. Like most brooms, it benefits from being clipped over after flowering to prevent it becoming leggy and likely to catch the wind.

Cytisus battandieri. From Morocco, this is an unusual and beautiful species for well-drained sunny places but is not hardy in really cold areas. It makes a tall shrub with greyish laburnum-like leaves and carries, in June, chubby upright racemes of canary-yellow flowers with a fruity pineapple scent. It is an ideal shrub for a sunny bank, and will occupy a space 1·7 by 2·5 m (6 by 8 ft).

Daphne. Some of the daphnes can be difficult. Some occasionally die out, but most are worth growing given the right conditions. Speaking personally, I would hate to be without the February to March flowering, purple *D. mezereum*—allow a 60 by 60 cm (2 by 2 ft) space—and its white variety 'Alba'. Particularly happy on chalk, they will grow in almost any garden, often securing their own immortality by means of seed. I find that most of the daphnes are happiest with a small stone slab or piece of slate over the root, and *D. mezereum* is no exception. Later-flowering, in May, *D. collina neapolitana*—allow a space 45 by 60 cm (18 in by 2 ft)—is a dwarf species with long-lasting rose-pink fragrant blooms. As with the early-blooming *D. mezereum*, the flowers are very fragrant. *D. × burkwoodii* is another good-value plant and semi-evergreen; from about 75 to 90 cm (2 ft 6 in to 3 ft) in height, it carries quantities of fragrant pale-pink flowers in May and June. Its taller growth and top hamper makes it liable to wind-rock and it should be well anchored with stones at planting time.

Desfontainea (for mild areas). This holly-like shrub is striking when decorated with its tubular scarlet, yellow-mouthed flowers. Blooming over a long period in late summer, it is a worthwhile shrub for the weekend gardener. It will not, however, grow on chalk and, like the crinodendron, prefers a moist rich soil in partial shade. *D. spinosa* 'Harold Comber' is the finest form. Slow growing, it attains a height and spread of 1·5 m (5 ft) in time.

Elaeagnus. The genus contains three foliage shrubs that are useful to the absent gardener. The first, *E. × ebbingei*—allow a space 2·5 by 2 m (8 by 6 ft)—makes a magnificent wind-break and is decorative with its silvery leaves; added to which it carries when established tiny fragrant flowers in autumn. The second, *E. macrophylla*, has silvered wavy-edged leaves and many fragrant flowers. like tiny ivory fuchsias, in autumn. It has a more spreading habit than *E. × ebbingei*—2·5 by 4 m (8 by 13 ft)—and is dense enough to make ground cover. However, it is less hardy than *E. × ebbingei*. It would be happy in the type of sunny 'commune' on well-drained soil where perovskia, cistus and phlomis thrive. The third variety, *E. pungens* 'Maculata', is a fine foliage shrub for winter effect with gold-splashed foliage that gives a wonderfully sunny effect. Allow a space 2·5 by 2 m (8 by 6 ft).

Embothrium, fire bush. Like the desfontainea and crinodendron, the embothrium comes from Chile and appreciates similar conditions on neutral-to-acid soil. With its tomato-scarlet honeysuckle-type flowers, it is the most brilliant shrub or small tree available to British gardeners. So bright is it, that it should be planted where it can be seen against the sky, given a stone or cream-washed building as background or set against green foliage. Contrast with other flowering subjects in close association can be disastrous. The Norquinco Valley form of *E. lanceolatum* is perfectly hardy. Keen winds can delay its flowering so it should be planted where some shelter is available. It will occupy a space 3 by 1·5 m (10 by 5 ft).

Erica. Several of the larger heaths flower over a considerable period and add a great deal to garden interest. Most need neutral-to-acid soil conditions but the late-winter-flowering *E.* × *darleyensis* (60 by 120 cm (2 by 4 ft)), the larger *E. mediterranea* (90 by 150 cm (3 by 5 ft)), and the August-September-blooming *E. stricta* (75 by 120 cm (2½ by 4 ft)) are lime tolerant.

On all soils the accommodating dwarf *E. carnea* forms will make pleasing carpets of winter colour, and can be used as ground cover. *E. c.* 'Springwood', however, is the most efficient at weed-suppression (see Chapter Three). For summer colour *E. vagans* 'Mrs D. F. Maxwell' still cannot be beaten, the 45 cm (18 in) hummocks becoming covered with long-lasting bottle-brush spikes of raspberry-pink, tan-anthered flowers at the end of July and carrying on into October. While *E. vagans* will not grow on chalk, we found it perfectly satisfactory in a previous garden on alkaline clay. The same was true of the *E.* × *watsonii* hybrid 'Dawn' which makes dense low clumps with yellow spring foliage and large, rose-pink bells throughout the late summer.

Of the tall, shrubby kinds which need an acid soil, *E. arborea* 'Alpina' makes an erect bush of about 1 m (3 to 4 ft) with fragrant, grey-white flowers in spring. For the rest of the year it is a pleasing hump of bright, mossy-green foliage. Its honey scent when in flower is so delightful and carrying that it well earns its place on that count alone.

Escallonia. This Chilean genus contains many good second-class shrubs, but only two or three that are outstanding. The flowers of most are long-lasting and can be so useful that the weekend gardener should not neglect them. They average about 1·4 to 2 m (4½ to 6½ ft) in height and are surprisingly lime-tolerant. Clipped over after flowering, many can be induced to give a late-autumn-to-winter display in mild areas. Most are not fully hardy away from the sea although those I shall name are reliable over most of southern and western Britain. 'Apple Blossom' is one of the best hybrids, slower-growing than most, with substantial pink and white bells of flower. 'Donard Brilliance' is a rich, rose-red, large-flowered shrub with a gracefully arching habit. 'Peach Blossom' is similar to 'Apple Blossom' and equally outstanding with peach-pink flowers, and 'Donard White' is a compact grower with white blossom opening from pinkish buds. The latter flowers over a particularly long period.

The glossily evergreen *E. macrantha* makes a fine seaside hedge and will be referred to again in Chapter Seven.

Eucalyptus. A genus of fast-growing, beautiful evergreen trees. Only one species, *E. parvifolia*, will grow on chalk soils, although many of the others are to be seen growing perfectly well on limestone. The main limitation, therefore, is climatic, and here the borderline is fine. Hardy along the south coast and much of southern Britain, I have seen eucalyptus species thriving in the west of Scotland, yet in North Wales their sites must be selected with care. Good air drainage and even wall shelter are required in some inland areas. On account of their suscep-tibility to damage from cold winds, the eucalyptus should be set out as pot-plants in spring. Wind-rock is also a danger and in exposed areas the trees may need to be guyed—wire passed through a rubber collar round the tree and fastened to tent pegs to windward, helping them to keep upright against the prevailing winds. It helps also to cut back young specimens that are making too rapid growth. Pruning even to 45 to 50 cm (18 to 20 in) from the ground can result in much stronger root anchorage. It then becomes necessary to select from the forest of young shoots the strongest to train as leader, removing all the other growth. Flower arrangers, however, may prefer to keep their plants bushy so as to be able to cut quantities of the attractive juvenile foliage. The hardiest and most generally accommodating species for the British Isles are: *E. dalrympleana* which makes a splendid small tree with an attractive patchwork bark that becomes white, and with grey-green leaves which are bronze when young; *E. gunnii*, the adult leaves of which are sickle-shaped and sage-green, has rounded, silver-blue leaves on its young shoots and is one of the most satisfactory species when kept regularly pruned to a large bush to yield cutting material—left to grow it forms a tall tree; *E. niphophila* which is slower-growing has large leathery, grey-green leaves and a patchwork trunk of grey, green and cream; *E. parvifolia*, mentioned earlier, is perhaps the hardiest of all, as well as the only one to grow well on chalky soils, and makes a medium-sized tree with narrow blue-green leaves.

Where they will grow, the eucalyptus form one of the most important decorative genera. A single tree can make a focal point of startling, year-round beauty, or a number can be grouped as with silver birches, and set in grass or sited to crown a small hillock.

Eucryphia. This genus is again less than universally hardy. The deciduous species *E. glutinosa* needs an acid soil but is valuable not only for the beauty of its large, single, white, rose-of-Sharon-type flowers, but for the glory of its autumn tints. It blooms throughout July and well into August, so even if one has the misfortune to miss its bloom, one would have to be away for a very long time to miss the autumn colour as well. Allow a space 2·5 by 2 m (about 8 by 6 ft). Of the evergreens the hybrid *E.* × *nymansensis* 'Mount Usher' is one of the best for general planting, forming a small, broadly columnar tree (2½ by 1·5 m (8 by 5 ft)) with large, fragrant flowers that are very freely borne in August and September. The well-known *E.* × *n.* 'Nymansay' is larger and even more rapid in growth, making an evergreen column of up to 6 m (20 ft) and having slightly larger flowers. All justify garden space and should succeed in reasonable shelter over southern and western Britain. The hybrids will grow even in limy soil.

Fabiana imbricata 'Prostrata'. The hardiest of this genus, it will succeed in sunny positions in moist, well-drained soil but will not grow on chalk. Flowering through May and June, when established it forms a mound of dense, feathery branches that become covered with blue-mauve tubular flowers. It has a 60 to 90 cm (2 to 3 ft) spread.

Forsythia. The best of these popular shrubs are the cultivars of *F.* × *intermedia*; 'Spectabilis', the upright, bright yellow form that is most commonly seen and the paler, softer-yellow variety known as 'Primulina'. The newer *F.* 'Lynwood' has fine flowers, but in our garden they do not last as well, while *F. suspensa* makes such a tangle of self-rooting growth that it can become a menace when one is not on hand to pinch out unwanted shoots. Like the flowering currant, the forsythia can help out the flower problem in town during the winter because branches cut on a visit to the garden can be taken back to open and bloom in water—a process which may take from two to three weeks. It requires a garden space of 1·8 by 1·5 m (6 by 5 ft).

Fuchsia. Valuable for all but the coldest gardens as permanent outdoor shrubs, some of the hybrids and species will last for years if planted a little deeper than normal or if the crowns of the plants are protected with ashes or dry peat before the start of the frosts. Their exceptionally long-flowering period makes them particularly suitable for the weekend gardener's use.

We find the best are: *F. magellanica* in its blush-flowered, 'Alba'

C

form; the common *F. m. gracilis* with scarlet and violet pendants; and *F. m.* 'Variegata' with striking foliage of green, margined with creamy yellow and flushed with pink. Unfortunately this last is less hardy than the type and should perhaps be grown against a wall. Both make sizeable bushes, in time reaching a height of 1·5 m (5 ft) with a spread of 1·5 to 2 m (about 5 to 7 ft).

Of the hybrids the large-flowered, scarlet-and-blue 'Mrs Popple', the scarlet-and-white small-growing 'Alice Hofman', the rose-and-violet 'Chillerton Beauty', and the semi-double crimson-and-violet 'Margaret' are the hardiest.

Garrya elliptica is a flower arranger's shrub—2·5 by 1·5 m (8 by 5 ft)—that is decorative in its own right, its long, tasselled catkins of pinky grey being carried throughout January and February. In cold areas it should be grown against a north- or east-facing wall. Elsewhere it can be grown as a bush in the open garden. It is particularly effective overhanging a bank.

Genista. This broom-like genus is valuable because it is lime-tolerant and offers several tall species that flower in the later summer, as well as supplying the excellent 45 cm (18 in) high *G. hispanica* for ground cover. Of the tall species, the finest is *G. aetnensis*, the Mount Etna broom, which makes an elegantly weeping specimen about 2 m (6 ft or more) high. This species is of slender growth and carries showers of tiny golden firefly flowers in July and August. Earlier to bloom is *G. cinerea* of similar habit, bearing a fragrant mass of golden-yellow blooms in June and July. *G. lydia* is a dwarf shrub with curving whorls of pendulous branchlets that become smothered with golden-yellow bloom in May. It will occupy a space 75 by 120 cm (2½ by 4 ft).

Hamamelis, witch hazel. The best winter-flowering subjects for neutral-acid soils. The spider-like yellow or orange-red flowers with maroon centres are borne in January and February and in the species *H. mollis* are beautifully scented. The golden-yellow *H. mollis* and the paler *H. m.* 'Pallida' are among the most generally useful. There is a newer hybrid, *H.* × *intermedia*, with taller more vigorous growth, the flowers of which unfortunately are less strongly scented. The best of these for garden effect are the orange 'Jelena' and the pale sulphur 'Moonlight' which are particularly effective in juxtaposition.

Hebe. This genus of evergreen New Zealand shrubs is particularly useful for seaside gardens. From among those which are reasonably hardy, the best are: the small-growing 'Autumn Glory' with continuously borne, densely packed violet racemes of bloom; *H.* × *franciscana* 'Blue Gem'; *H.* × *f.* 'Variegata', the leaves of which are edged with cream; 'Great Orme' with long racemes of bright pink flowers in summer, and the lavender-flowered 'Midsummer Beauty'. These make dome-shaped bushes of 60 to 90 cm (2 to 3 ft).

Hippophae rhamnoides, sea buckthorn. A valuable shrub for difficult exposed gardens and fine for seaside planting. It must be grouped to ensure the production of berries as the individual plants are unisexual. Deciduous, its silvery, narrow leaves are attractive in summer and its orange-yellow berries remain for a long time in winter as their acrid juice makes them unpalatable to birds. It will occupy a space 90 by 120 cm (3 by 4 ft).

Hydrangea. This genus is one of those likely to give most pleasure to the absent gardener, as the species and hybrids remain in flower for such an exceptionally long time. Most bloom in late summer and into the autumn and although they are not all hardy enough for the coldest gardens, *H. paniculata* 'Grandiflora' will grow anywhere and is extremely decorative with its massive plume-shaped panicles made up of large florets, which open green, turn to white and fade into pink. For the finest flowers it should be pruned back to within a few inches of the previous year's growth. Of the familiar mop-headed Hortensia varieties which colour pink on limy soils and blue on acid, with many shades of mauve and purple intervening, the hardiest are 'Hamburg', 'Generale Vicomtesse de Vibraye', and 'Deutschland'. 'Altona' with huge heads of fimbriated florets is the finest, large-growing variety for seaside use and for planting in mild areas. For small gardens the dwarf 'Vulcan', 'Munster', and 'Miss Belgium' are more suitable. In informal areas of the garden, the lace-cap forms with showy infertile florets surrounding the bead-like fertile heads are most attractive. They are good too in flower arrangements and, like all hydrangeas, last well if cut between two nodes with the stem then being slit upwards for several inches through the node above. Sizes vary from 30 cm to over 2 m (1 to 6 or 8 ft) in height with a comparable spread. On limy soils, hydrangeas may suffer from chlorosis (yellowing of the leaf) but may be treated with Murphy Sequestrene to correct this. To obtain good blue shades in neutral soils, half a kilogram (1 lb) of commercial alum per four stems should be spread over the root area of the plant in autumn and allowed to wash in with the winter rains.

Hypericum. The species *H. calycinum* has been dealt with under ground cover in Chapter Three. Of the remainder, the shrubby 'Hidcote' is the best for general planting. Of mounded habit, it will reach about 1·5 m (5 ft) in height with a spread of about 2 m (6 ft) or more. Its large golden flowers are particularly effective next to a blue-flowered hydrangea or caryopteris. It should be sheared after flowering to retain a dense compact form. The main burst of bloom comes in

June-July and if sheared afterwards, this will often be followed by a second flowering in October. Otherwise there will be sporadic attempts at bloom throughout the summer.

Ilex, holly. Of dual purpose on account of their year-round greenery and berries, it is in their variegated forms that the hollies reach their greatest ornamental value. *I* × *clarensis* 'Golden King' is undoubtedly the best golden variegated form and, being female in spite of its name, will berry well if there is a male or bisexual form nearby. Paradoxically *I. aquifolium* 'Golden Queen' is a male that can be relied on to perform the pollinating function. Otherwise one can choose the white-margined *I. a.* 'Silver Queen' (male). The nomenclature of the hollies is always a trap for the unwary as whoever bestowed the cultivar names must have been singularly unaware of the basic facts of heterosexual life!

The best all-green variety is *I. aquifolium* 'J. C. van Tol' with shiny dark, almost spineless, green leaves. Fortunately this variety is bisexual and can be relied not only to berry without a pollinator but to pollinate nearby female plants. Slow-growing, the hollies should be allowed a space about 2 by 2 m (6 by 6 ft). They can, however, be kept more compact by clipping.

Itea ilicifolia. An unusual late-summer-blooming shrub, it enjoys half-shade. It is worth planting for its drooping racemes of fragrant greeny-white flowers. Of lax appearance, its foliage is holly-like and evergreen. The catkins last a long time and it is well worth its space in the week-ender's garden. It will occupy an area 2·5 by 2 m (8 by 6 ft approx.).

Jasminum nudiflorum, winter jasmine. Whether grown against a wall trained to wires or allowed to form a free-rambling mound in the border, this is among the very best of winter-flowering shrubs. Its primrose, starry blooms are carried over a very long period, opening in frost-free spells from November to March. They open well in water.

Jovellana violacea. A semi-hardy shrub for a warm terrace or house wall, it bears mauve calceolaria-like flowers in June and July and will occupy a space 120 by 90 cm (4 by 3 ft).

Kerria. Useful for cold or alkaline soils, the kerria is well known for its double, golden pom-poms of bloom. It is usually grown against a wall and should be ordered under the name *Kerria japonica* 'Pleniflora'. The less-well-known, single-flowered type is attractive as a bush in the border; its gracefully arching branches carry large buttercup-like single golden blooms. Flowering in April and May its bare green stems are also attractive in winter. It needs a space of 1·8 by 1·2 m (6 by 4 ft).

Laburnum. Most people like to have a laburnum in the garden and the golden yellow racemes usually last quite a long time in beauty. The hybrid *L.* × *watereri* 'Vossii' has the longest chains of bloom and, being upright in habit, can easily be trained to form an arch—two, four, six or more specimens being used on either side. The 'Aureum' form of the common *L. anagyroides* is worth planting in addition because its soft-yellow leaves retain their colour throughout the summer. Sometimes this form is apt to revert to the normal green so a watch should be kept for any stray shoots which should be cut out when they make their appearance. Allow an area about 3 by 3 m (10 by 10 ft).

Lavandula, lavender. A favourite among aromatic shrubs, the lavender needs a well-drained soil in sun. Provided they are sheared over in early spring the shrubs retain a compact habit and do not become straggly. Failure to shear results in overgrown bushes which break off and rapidly deteriorate. 'Alba' is the well-known greyish-white lavender which flowers in late July and grows to 60 to 90 cm (2 to 3 ft). It is particularly effective in a border of blue, mauve and grey colourings. 'Vera' is the Dutch lavender, the robust lavender-blue-flowered counterpart of 'Alba', while 'Hidcote' is the best dwarf form reaching up to 45 cm (18 in), and carrying many dense-packed spikes. *L. stoechas*, the unusual Mediterranean lavender, is worth growing in warm, dry, sunny spots for the strongly aromatic scent of its foliage and its tufted, congested heads of dark purple.

Lespedeza thunbergii. A broom-like shrub with arching stems weighed down by large panicles of small pea-like rose-purple flowers in September. It lasts in bloom for a considerable time and is most accommodating if given full sun. Bushes reach a height of around 1 m (3 ft) and have a similar, but rather thin, spread.

Lithospermum diffusum 'Heavenly Blue'. One of the glories of neutral-to-acid soils, blooming in spring and early summer. A dwarf shrublet, we grow ours at the front of the later-blooming *Erica vagans* 'Mrs D. F. Maxwell' and the lithospermum climbs through the heath to enrich its dark foliage with brilliant blue stars, thus giving two season of colour to the same area.

Lonicera. Of the shrubby forms of the honeysuckle genus, *L. nitida* 'Baggessen's Gold' makes a valuable coloured-foliage subject. It reaches about 1·4 m (4½ ft), and stands clipping well. Of the climbers the early Dutch, *L. periclymenum* 'Belgica' is the longest lasting for flower and scent. Thought must be taken before planting the rampant *L. japonica halliana* within reach of any choice shrubs or roses. In our garden it proved an ineradicable climber on which we had to wage merciless war before it choked the much better and more rewarding subjects it invaded.

Magnolia. For the weekend gardener some of the hybrids of the *M.* × *soulangiana* group are the best value. In North Wales we grew the upright-habited 'Picture' which flowered over a long season in spring and usually bore a fair crop of autumn blooms. The vase-shaped, waxy blooms are rose-to-purple on the outside and white within. Ours bloomed within a year of planting. The more spreading 'Lennei' has a similarly long period of interest but its flowers are quite different and most striking—rounded goblets that are solidly coloured rose-purple on the outside and white streaked with soft purple within. In addition to these two magnolias the summer-blooming *M. sieboldii* is worth growing on acid soils. This species bears nodding white, lemon-scented flowers with its leaves from May to August. Never spectacular, the sporadic nature of its blooming means that there are almost always some of its attractive flowers to be enjoyed when one returns to the garden, and the scent permeates the whole area. It will grow to some 3 m (10 ft) with a spread of 2·5 to 3·7 m (8 to 12 ft).

Mahonia. Apart from the ground-covering mahonias referred to in Chapter Three, there are two spectacular winter-blooming shrubs with foliage that is handsome throughout the year. Both should be planted for a succession of bloom from October to February. The hybrid 'Charity' opens its fragrant, deep-yellow racemes first and these are borne like upright, spreading cockades, quite different from the laxly drooping, primrose-yellow blooms of *M. japonica* which can usually be relied on to bloom at Christmas and well into the new year. Both have magnificent pinnate leaves that colour with tones of scarlet and crimson during the winter months, and will occupy a space 1·8 by 1·8 m (6 by 6 ft).

Malus. The ornamental crabs have two seasons of beauty. Flowering well in spring, they bear colourful fruit in autumn. Some of the best for both purposes are the pale-pink-flowered 'Cashmere' with its yellow apples, 'Chilko' with purple-red flowers and shiny crimson fruit, and 'Crittenden' with pale-pink blossom and scarlet fruit (all three may be purchased from Hilliers of Winchester), while for blossom alone and coppery young leaves 'Profusion' is perhaps the most widely distributed. It makes a fine small tree with showy scarlet-crimson flowers, occupying a space of some 2·5 by 3 m (8 by 10 ft).

Mutisia. *M. oligodon* is a delightful scrambler with shiny, slightly recurving, petalled flowers like large pink daisies, which can ramble through and decorate any low hummocky shrubs. *M. ilicifolia* is similar but taller, and vigorous enough to scramble over hardy fuchsias, cistuses and shrubs of similar habit. Again, both are obtainable from Hilliers of Winchester. Neither would be satisfactory in cold areas, but they succeed, even inland, in North Wales. They flower continuously over a long period.

Passiflora caerulea, passion flower. Another climber which, like the clematis and mutisia, can be used to bring a second season of flowering to early shrubs, or an earlier season to a late-blooming species. It is normally in flower about midsummer.

Perovskia (see also p. 88). *P. atriplicifolia* is a late-flowering sun-lover, which appreciates a well-drained soil and full sun. Its misty-blue flowers, grey foliage and white stems make it ideal for the sunny border, or to form part of a sun-loving 'commune' on a raised bed or bank. It lasts in beauty for a considerable time and even before it flowers in August its foliage adds considerably to the general border effect. Dying back in winter, in summer it makes a silvery spire of about 1·2 m (4 ft). The old spikes should be left on the plant over the winter period and in spring cut back to about 45 cm (18 in) from the ground.

Philadelphus, mock orange. This is a genus which few gardeners would like to be without. As with most genera, the double-flowered cultivars tend to last longer in bloom than the single. Even so, I would not dismiss the superb, compact 'Belle Etoile' with its large, squarish, purple-centred blooms that have a fresh, uncloying fragrance like Orange Pekoe tea. This variety makes a mounded bush of 1·2 m (4 ft) or so. Of the doubles, 'Albatre' is one of the most free in flower and not too gaunt and tall in growth. It will succeed almost anywhere, as will the better known and more vigorous 'Virginal' (2 by 1·2 m (about 6 by 4 ft)).

Phlomis fruticosa. This has been dealt with as a ground-covering subject in Chapter Three. It does well on any well-drained, sunny bank and is attractive on account of its grey-green leaves and whorls of long lasting golden flowers. It has a relative in *P*. 'Edward Bowles', a small, front-row sub-shrub with large, heart-shaped, hairy-looking leaves and whorls of pretty sulphur-yellow flowers throughout late summer and autumn. Like *P. fruticosa*, 'Edward Bowles' is hardy in all but the coldest districts. Allow a garden space of 75 to 90 cm (2½ to 3 ft) by 120 cm (4 ft).

Pieris. A member of the *Ericaceae* and needing lime-free soil, *P.* 'Forest Flame' is one of the best of all shrubs. Hardy, always attractive in leaf, it is at its peak in spring when the brilliant-red, young growths are followed by drooping panicles of creamy-white lily-of-the-valley-type flowers. Later, the young leaves pale to rose and then become creamy before assuming their normal green. The scarlet and rose colouring often persists as late as June, giving a very long season of interest. Slow-growing, it will eventually occupy a space 3 by 2½ m (about 10 by 8 ft).

Potentilla. A genus which offers some of the most worthwhile small shrubs for the average garden. The various forms of *P. fruticosa* average 90 to 120 cm (3 to 4 ft) in height, and flower from May to September. They will thrive in any soil but flower best in full sun. A hard cutting-back in spring aids flowering and helps to keep the bushes compact. Among the best are the deep-yellow 'Buttercup', the taller 'Farrer's White', 'Friedrichsenii' with grey-green foliage and light-yellow flowers, 'Lady Daresbury' with large yellow flowers borne in two main flushes in spring and autumn. 'Primrose Beauty', and the more unusual 'Sunset', 'Daydawn' and 'Tangerine', the orange and pale coppery-yellow flowers of which associate so well with the misty blue of caryopteris to make a valuable border association. For those who like it and don't mind spending an extra two or three pounds to secure a patented plant, there is also the new and eye-catching 'Red Ace'.

Prunus. The ornamental cherries are so lovely that most gardeners like to plant at least one specimen in their gardens. Many, however, are too fleeting in their effect for the weekend gardener's purpose. The longest-lasting are the pink 'Fugenzo', 'Shimidsui'—a late, frilly, double white—and 'Shirofugen', which is even later in bloom and has pale-blush flowers and coppery young leaves. We prolong their season by growing through them the thornless sweetly-scented climbing rose 'Zephirine Drouhin' with its rich pink, informal flowers. The autumn-winter blooming *Prunus subhirtella autumnalis* 'Rosea' is worth a place, as it flowers during any mild spells throughout the winter and if cut in bud will open indoors. Allow a space 2·5 to 3 m (8 to 10 ft) by 3 to 4·5 m (10 to 15 ft).

Pyracantha, firethorn. A very hardy genus, the members of which can either be grown against walls or as shrubs in the open ground. The only drawback is that the birds avidly devour the berries of some species, including the favourite *P. coccinea* 'Lalandei', almost as soon as ripe. The winter-ripening sorts and the yellow-berried forms usually last much longer in fruit. For prolonged effect the best are *P. angustifolia* which has conspicuous clusters of orange-yellow fruits that last all winter, and *P. atalantoides* which ripens late and will do well even in a sunless position, together with its yellow-fruited 'Aurea' variety, which is long-lasting in berry. A hybrid known as 'Buttercup' did extremely well with us on a steep bank where its spreading habit was an attraction. It bore quantities of small rich-yellow fruits, while its young spring leaves are attractively bronzed, making it a first-class companion for its neighbour, the rich blue-flowered *Caenothus* 'Edinburgh'. Against a wall, allow a space 1·5 to 6 m (5 to 20 ft) by 2·5 m (8 ft).

Pyrus salicifolia 'Pendula'. The silver-leafed weeping pear makes a graceful small tree that is beautiful from the time its buds open until its narrow silver leaves turn yellow and fall. The fruit is barely edible but the white blossom is pretty and the foliage effect delightful. In time this pear makes a tree of some 2 to 2·5 m (6 to 8 ft) in height with a spread of about 2·5 m (8 ft).

Rhododendron. Whether or not this beautiful family is worth the absent gardener's while is for the individual to decide. I can only point out that while the blossom of many of the large, mid-season hybrids is fleeting, the earliest to bloom last quite a long time in flower, and where a selection is grown one would have to be unlucky indeed to miss the blooming of them all. For gardens that miss the worst of the spring frosts, such hybrids as the February-flowering 'Praecox' with its pinky-purple, azalea-type blooms, the later 'Blue Tit', 'Sapphire', 'Blue Diamond', pink 'Tessa', and some of the dwarf species such as *impeditum*, *chryseum*, *scintillans*, *hancenaum* 'Nanum', *myrtilloides*, and *sargentianum* could be mixed with the dwarf evergreen azaleas and some of the taller double Ghent azalea varieties such as the pale-yellow 'Narcissiflorum', the pale-pink 'Raphael de Smet', the warm-pink 'Norma' and the newer pink 'Homebush', to form an island bed that, regularly mulched, will give little trouble and have a long season of beauty, extended by the autumn-foliage colour of the deciduous azaleas and the winter tints of the dwarfs. *R. chryseum* has interesting bronzy foliage for much of the year, that of *R. impeditum* is frosty grey and the June-flowering *R. charitopes* could be added for the attraction of its plum-speckled blossom and glaucous foliage. Sizes vary from the lowly 45 by 60 cm (18 by 24 in) spread of *R. pemakoense* to the larger hybrids which in time reach 2 to 2·5 m (about 6 to 8 ft) or more in height and spread. (For further information see Chapter Six).

Salix. Apart from *S. babylonica*, the weeping willow, which can only be grown where there is sufficient room, much of the attraction of the genus lies in the catkins. Long-lasting in late winter and spring, the smaller willows are worth the weekend gardener's space, and it is pleasant to cut a sheaf of 'pussies' to take back to town after a country break. The shrubby *S. gracilistyla* (1·5 by 1·5, (about 5 by 5 ft)) is one of the earliest and best, or the delightful *S. purpurea* 'Pendula' (1·5 × 2m, (about 5 × 6 ft)), grown as a weeping standard, might be chosen. I like to grow also *S. repens argentea*, the dwarf creeping willow, with its silky, silvery leaves and tiny catkins which open to showy 'fluffy ducklings' of yellow in spring.

Salvia. See Chapter Three.

Santolina. See Chapter Three.

Sarcococca. Of this genus, the species *S. humilis* is the one most worth growing by weekend gardeners, a dwarf shrub that makes effective ground cover and is at the same time valuable in the winter garden for the scent of its tiny white flowers and the fresh beauty of its small shining leaves; a small bunch will scent a room. It is particularly useful in that it will grow on any type of soil, including chalk, occupying a space 45 by 60 cm (1½ by 2 ft).

Senecio greyi is useful ground cover for a sunny bank and as such is mentioned in Chapter Three. It is also a valuable subject for the large flower border or shrub planting. Its silvery-grey leaves associate well with most plants and its sunny 'daisies' blend in easily. However, those who dislike the flowers can shear the bush over while in bud. In any case it should be clipped after flowering in order to keep a dense, compact shape (1·2 by 2 m (about 4 by 6 ft)). *S. cineraria* is a soft-stemmed plant often used in bedding schemes for the elegance of its deeply cut silver leaves. In milder areas it will withstand the winter, but the blooms of this species are decidedly mustardy, and I prefer to remove the buds before they open. The foliage is particularly useful to set off blue, pink or mauve flowers. Allow a space 60 by 70 cm (2 by 2½ ft).

Skimmia. Useful mainly for the effect of its berries, its foliage is also quietly handsome and its heads of small, starry white flowers in spring give off a delicious fragrance. *S.* 'Foremanii' is the best in fruit but it needs a pollinator, which function might well be undertaken by the especially sweetly scented male form of *S. japonica*, 'Fragrans'. Allow a space 75 by 90 cm (2½ by 3 ft).

Solanum crispum 'Glasnevin'. Usually seen as a wall plant that needs the support of wires or mesh, It can equally well be grown as a freely rambling bush on a warm border in full sun. Semi-evergreen, it carries its blue-mauve potato-flowers in loose corymbs from July to September, and is good in association with musk roses such as the coppery-pink 'Cornelia' or the warm-pink 'Felicia'. It should be kept away from the truer blues of ceanothus or ceratostigma, but looks well with *Spartium junceum* (Spanish broom), yellow roses, or the purple-foliaged *Cotinus coggygria* 'Royal Purple'. Allow a space 1·5 by 1 m (5 by 3 ft).

Sorbus. The various cultivars of this genus, which includes *S. aucuparia*, the mountain ash, are available for their autumn berries and leaf-colour. *S. aucuparia* 'Edulis' carries heavy bunches of large, sweetly edible fruits which make excellent rowanberry jelly. Yellow-berried forms, such as 'Xanthocarpa', are less attractive to the birds than the more scarlet-orange and so last longer in beauty. They reach a height of up to 4·5 m (15 ft) with a comparable spread. *S. cashmiriana* is a particular favourite of mine with its pretty heads of pale-pink flowers in May and large, white, glistening berries that remain long after the leaves have fallen. The yellow-fruited 'Ethel's Gold' also lasts well in berry—often until the New Year, while another good form is *S. aucuparia* 'Fastigiata', slow-growing and columnar in habit, a first-class tree for the smaller garden with large, sealing-wax-red fruits that ripen late and usually last well. Allow a space 2 by 1 m (about 6 by 3 ft).

Spartium junceum, Spanish broom. A strong-growing shrub that needs pruning back occasionally in March to keep it compact. Care must be taken, as with all the broom family, not to cut into the old wood. The spartium carries showy upright racemes of comparatively large, golden pea-flowers throughout the summer and early autumn and is remarkable for the strong narcissus-like scent of its blossom. Hardy in most southern and western districts, in colder areas it should be given a sunny. well-drained place. It is an excellent seaside shrub, and will occupy a space 2 by 2·5 m (about 6 by 8 ft).

Spiraea. Most valuable for the weekend gardener is the hybrid *S.* × *bumalda* of which the crimson-flowered dwarf 'Anthony Waterer' is the best for general effect as it remains in flower for quite a long period. Usually about 60 to 90 cm (2 to 3 ft) high, it has a rival in the densely compact *S. japonica* 'Alpina'—45 cm (18 in) high—with its heads of rosy pink. This latter is effective when massed at the front of a flower border. The plants should be set 45 cm (18 in) or so apart.

Syringa. Of the lilacs, the double forms last longest in flower, the old favourite white *S. vulgaris* 'Madame Lemoine' seeming particularly durable. Weekend gardeners with space to spare should plant a succession of varieties to be sure of catching at least one at its peak. Early-flowering lavender-purple *S. v.* 'Katharine Havemeyer' and the later-blooming claret-rose *S. v.* 'Paul Thirion', both double-flowered, should, with *S. v.* 'Madame Lemoine', meet the case. Allow a space 2·5 by 1·5 m (about 8 by 5 ft).

Ulex europaeus 'Plenus'. Our native gorse is a superb shrub for country gardens or for the seaside, its golden, semi-double flowers smother the bush throughout April and May. It is a good wind-resister and makes an excellent low wind-break, reaching up to 1½ m (5 ft) if clipped.

Viburnum. One of the most useful garden genera, the season starts in October with the long-blooming, fragrant *V.* × *bodnantense* (2·5 by 2 m (8 by 6 ft)), which will flower the winter through during mild spells. In April there follows the neat, bushy *V.* × *juddii* (120 by 90 cm (4 by 3 ft)) with apple-blossom heads of sweet-smelling, pink-tinged white flowers. Accompanying it and carrying on until June, there is the larger-growing *V.* × *carlcephalum* (2 by 2.5 m (about 6 by 8 ft)) with rounder, more globular heads. Perhaps the finest of all, and a most useful shrub for ground cover, is the low-growing *V. plicatum* 'Rowallane' (90 to 120 cm (3 to 4 ft) by 180 cm (6 ft)) with flat creamy heads, like those of lace-cap hydrangeas, which smother the tiered branches in May. This variety lasts in beauty with us for three full weeks. Both 'Rowallane' and the type, the snowball-flowered *V. plicatum* colour well in autumn. *V. tinus* (2·5 by 3 m (about 8 by 10 ft)), the laurustinus, is an evergreen that blooms from late autumn to spring in all but the coldest areas. For small gardens its more compact form, 'Eve Price', is the most useful with attractive carmine buds and pink-tinged flowers.

Weigela. A useful summer-flowering genus with one or two outstandingly decorative members. Among these are two exceptionally good foliage shrubs in the cultivars of *W. florida*; one is known as 'Foliis Purpureis' with small rose-pink flowers against bronze-purple leaves that retain their colour throughout the season; the other is 'Variegata' which has larger, paler-pink flowers that deepen to rose as they fade, and cream-edged leaves.

Both are extremely valuable border shrubs. In our own garden we grow them among herbaceous plants, finding that a stiffening of shrubs in the border helps to obviate the need for staking, while the foliage colour helps to set off other plants. The variegated weigela associates particularly well with delphiniums, the double hardy *Geranium pratense* 'Caerulea' and the recurrently flowering Bourbon rose 'Louis Odier', while the purple-leafed form is attractive if grouped with silver-foliaged *Senecio cineraria*, pink Chinese paeonies, Japanese anemones and white regale lilies. Many of the hardy hybrid weigelas can be induced to flower again in autumn, if the flowered shoots are shortened or removed as soon as the blossom fades. Showiest of these are the rose-pink 'Conquête' and 'Bristol Ruby' with flowers of a brighter red than the better-known 'Eva Rathke', 'Buisson Fleuri', obtainable from Hilliers, is also attractive and is early in bloom with scented rose-pink flowers that are spotted with yellow in the throat. Apart from these we grow the species *W. middendorffiana*, a shrub of considerable quality, which is less hardy than the 'toughies' so far mentioned and should be given a sheltered and partially shaded place where its yellow foxglove-like blooms will make a lasting show. The weigelas make bushes 1·2 to 1·5 m (about 4 to 5ft) in height and spread.

CONIFERS FOR LASTING COLOUR EFFECT

Chamaecyparis.. This conifer will grow on any soil including chalk, although there it will make slower growth. The genus offers a considerable variety of evergreen colour and a varied habit of growth, ranging from the slow-growing *C. lawsoniana* 'Aurea Densa' which will eventually reach 2 m (6 ft or more) with close-packed, golden-yellow fans of foliage, to the tall *C. l.* 'Wisselii' with its fern-like sprays of bluey-green. In between are numerous other forms, of which the best are the medium-sized, golden 'Winston Churchill'; the large, glaucous 'Triomf de Boskoop'; the large, cone-shaped, golden 'Stewartii'; the dwarf 'Pygmae Argentea' with dark, bluey-green foliage tipped with white; the columnar, sea-green 'Pottenii'; the feathery, dwarf yellow 'Minima Aurea'; 'Kilmacurragh' which is the best to simulate the tender Mediterranean cypress in effect, as it makes a similar dark green column; and the compact, dense, grey-green 'Fletcheri' which makes a column eventually reaching 5·5 m (18 ft). The *C. pisifera* forms are also distinct with their flattened sprays of foliage and broad, conical habit. Among them is the attractive and slow-growing 'Filifera Aurea' with long, drooping sprays of thin golden foliage.

Ginkgo biloba, the maidenhair tree. With its small, fan-shaped leaves that give it the appearance of a giant maidenhair fern, this deciduous conifer is sufficiently compact for most gardens. It is distinctive and beautiful enough to be given a focal place, and is quite outstanding in its soft yellow autumn colouring. Quite hardy, it is fortunately suitable for most types of soil.

Juniperus is one of the most useful conifer genera, as it is excellent on chalk and comprises both tall, striking growers and dwarf, spreading forms that are ideal for weed-suppression (these latter forms have been dealt with in Chapter Three).

Of the taller cultivars. *J. chinensis* 'Aurea' makes a tall, slender column of golden yellow, while 'Columnaris Glauca' is similar but shorter in growth, with glaucous foliage. *J. communis* offers the dwarf slow-growing 'Compressa', the Noah's ark tree, and the dense, columnar 'Hibernica', the Irish juniper, which grows up to 4 or 4·2 m (13 or 14 ft) and is sometimes used as a substitute for the Italian cypress when designing colder British gardens. *J. c.* 'Hibernica' has been used in this way with notable effect at Portmeirion, Sir Clough Williams-Ellis's famous Italian model village in North Wales. Another fine and very distinct juniper is 'Grey Owl', which makes a vigorous, medium-sized shrub with spreading branches and soft but spiky silver-grey foliage.

ROSES FOR THE WEEKEND GARDEN

As with shrubs and trees, the absent gardener needs roses that will remain in flower for a long time, preferably 'die' well—not retaining masses of faded disfiguring blooms—and be to some extent capable of looking after themselves.

Few of the hybrid teas and floribundas fall into this category, but the best varieties for the purpose are the most vigorous ones such as the old pink-and-gold 'Shot Silk' which if lightly pruned makes a large shrubby bush, ideal to grow among flowers in the mixed border and carrying at least three prolonged flushes of bloom during the season. 'Chinatown', which is in effect a smaller-bloomed 'Peace', does well when grown in this fashion, so do 'Iceberg', 'Pink Favourite', 'My Choice', 'Queen Elizabeth', 'Chicago Peace', and 'Fervid'. Pillar roses such as the scarlet single 'Dortmund' which in our district in North Wales was pest- and disease-free, 'Golden Showers', and the double bright-red 'Danse du Feu' may equally well be grown as shrubs. Recurrently flowering, they are sturdy enough, yet sufficiently light in foliage to act as hosts to the hybrid clematis. We had the blue-purple *Clematis* 'Jackmanii Superba' scrambling through 'Golden Showers' with remarkable effect, and the pale blue *Clematis* 'Mrs Cholmondely' or double white *C.* 'Duchess of Edinburgh' are spectacular to accompany the rose 'Danse du Feu'.

Earlier pillar roses that are suitable to be grown as shrubs include the pink 'Aloha', the dark-red 'Guinée', and the peachy-orange 'Schoolgirl'.

Apart from these, if looked at purely as shrubs, the Japanese rugosa roses have much to recommend them. Hardy, tolerant of any conditions from chalk to acid heathland, or even pure sand, they make mounded bushes with handsome bright-green foliage that colours to corn-yellow in autumn. They are continually in flower, particularly if the early fruits are snipped off while in the green stage, and bear large, vivid, tomato-shaped fruits in autumn. Their blooms are large, single or informally double, often beautiful in bud, and sweetly fragrant. Of these paragons, the best to my mind are the white semi-double 'Blanc Double de Coubert', pale-rose-pink single 'Frau Dagmar Hastrop', crimson-purple double 'Roseraie de l'Hay', and 'Schneezwerg' which should never be dead-headed as the comparatively small orange-scarlet fruits are most effective when carried among the later, heavy crops of snowy flowers. Mixed seedlings of *Rosa rugosa* may also be planted at 60 cm (2 ft) apart to make a dense and pleasing hedge. They are attractive in autumn when their vivid hips contrast with the golden yellow of their fading leaves. A rugosa hedge will be quite wind-resistant. It should be clipped lightly after the first flowering and may be cut back harder during winter or spring. The rugosa roses are notable in that they never seem to become victims to either mildew or black spot, although they may occasionally suffer from light attacks of aphis which, however, do not seem able to do much harm to their tough buds and stems. They make bushes of up to 1·5 m (5 ft) with a 2 m (about 6ft)-spread. (See also p. 49.)

Another group of roses worth the weekend gardener's attention is that of the musk hybrids, delightful in scent and almost perpetual in flower. Of these the soft pink 'Felicia', pink and white 'Penelope', apricot 'Buff Beauty', semi-double white 'Pax', orange-scarlet 'Berlin', and pinky-apricot 'Cornelia' are the best and also the most easily obtainable. Specialist nurseries such as David Austin Ltd, Albrighton, Wolverhampton, usually carry stocks. Unlike the rugosa roses, the musk hybrids need the usual precautionary spraying either with Maneb and Karathane against black spot, mildew and rust, or with the systemic Benlate. Grown as laxly spreading bushes, they are generous with their smallish but delightful and often well-shaped flowers, and may in time reach to almost 2 m (6 ft) in height with rather less spread.

Modern shrub roses worth growing—either in grass, among border flowers, or among other shrubs—are the single pink 'Ballerina'; the single 'First Choice' in scarlet and gold; multi-coloured 'Jospeh's Coat' and semi-double, scarlet 'Will Scarlett'.

To these may be added the ground-covering 'Max Graf' with its fragrant, rose-pink blooms on long, trailing stems, and 'Temple Bells'. Both these varieties flower only once but over a very long period, and they are attractive for clothing a difficult bank.

HERBACEOUS PLANTS FOR THE WEEKEND GARDEN

In gardens where the owner cannot always be on hand to water, stake, and generally come to the rescue in times of emergency, perennials no less than shrubs and trees must be of the type able to fend for themselves, given reasonable soil preparation and mulching care. They should be sturdy and preferably dwarf so as to require no staking, and they should not be prone to collapse in prolonged periods of sunny drought. If a favourite perennial is lost, its replacement may take several years to establish itself to the point where it satisfactorily takes the place of the original plant, so the initial plantings must be carefully chosen. The following list should be helpful.

Acanthus spinosus. A distinguished foliage plant with handsome, deeply cut leaves and pleasing spires of purplish-white flowers reaching up to 1·2 m (4ft), it blooms effectively from June to August. It is substantial enough not to need support unless grown in very exposed sites. When staking is needed it can be unobtrusively provided by metal ring supports set in position in spring. These will be quickly disguised by the foliage.

Achillea. The flat-headed 'Moonshine' has the most pleasing colour in this sun-loving genus. The stems rise only to 60 cm (2 ft) and so need no support, and the dense, grey leaves are attractive. The plant is in flower from May to July and sometimes later, but needs full sun to give of its best.

Agapanthus Headbourne Hybrids. In all but the coldest gardens they form strong clumps growing to 45 cm (18 in) or more. They love the sun and are drought-resistant to a marked degree, but to do well they should be surrounded by a generous mulch of moist peat or compost in April. Soaked, rolled newspapers or well-soaked peat dug into the planting hole is also a help in enabling them to resist drought in later years. If possible they should be given deep, well-drained soil, and will do well in front of shrubs where overhanging leaves will not prevent the rain reaching them. Their variously shaded blue, lily-like flowers make them among the best of border plants.

Alchemilla mollis. (See also Chapter Three.) This is a fine plant for flower arranging, ground cover and sheer border worth. Moreover it is trouble free. It should be planted at the front where the beauty of its softly pleated, green leaves and yellow-green sprays of fluffy flowers (reaching a height of 45 cm, (18 in)) can be appreciated. Set 45 cm (18 in) apart.

Anaphalis. Any of the available species are useful for poor, dry soil. Their silver-grey foliage is attractive and their heads of small white, helichrysum-like flowers are everlasting and can be dried for use with other immortelles for indoor decoration during the winter months. I would particularly recommend *A. margaritacea*, whilst the best and most effective species for ground cover is *A. triplinervis*, which attains about 30 cm (12 in) in height. Set 45 cm (18 in) apart.

Anemone hupehensis and hybrids. The original Japanese anemones are reliable, late-summer-to-autumn-flowering perennials that ask little beyond a reasonably good soil, preferably in sunshine. Almost all are good, but the best and most free-flowering over a long period are 'Luise Uhink' (white), 'Bressingham Glow' (pink, semi-double) and 'Kriemhilde' (clear pink and extra sturdy, low growth).

A. vitifolia (see also Chapter Three), which tolerates shade better than the hybrids, comes into flower earlier and tends to spread itself through the border by rhizomatous self-propagation.

All remain in flower for several weeks and need no support, reaching a height of 60 to 90 cm (2 to 3 ft). Set 60 cm (2 ft) apart.

Anthemis, chamomile. *A. cupaniana* has already been recommended as a ground-covering plant for well-drained sunny places (see Chapter Three) where its finely cut silver foliage and succession of white marguerite-type 'daises' render it useful for most of the year. *A. sancti-johannis* is much more accommodating with regard to soil and climate. It seldom exceeds 45 cm (18 in) and needs no staking, but it must have full sun. Bushy in habit and freely-branching, its stems of orange-yellow 'daisies' are produced over many weeks. It should be cut back in September to assist perennial growth, and requires about the same spacing as the anaphalis and alchemilla. *A. tinctoria* 'Mrs E. C. Buxton' is another fine plant, bearing lemon-yellow flowers over a long period. It should be given a base of well-soaked peat at planting time—or folded, well-soaked newspapers—otherwise its stems may become bare of foliage during a dry season. *A. t.* 'Mrs Buxton' is a front-to-middle-row plant with a spread of about 75 cm (2 ft 6 in).

Antholyza paniculata (see *Curtonus paniculatus*)

Aquilegia. The well-loved columbine is worth a place in any garden. Individual plants do not flower over a long period, but if grouped their flowering will spread over some time. Moreover, the columbines often seed themselves and, taking up little space, are a pleasant addition to any border. The best strain available is still 'McKana Hybrids' which reach 90 cm (3 ft) but need no staking. Set 45 cm (18 in) apart.

Armeria, thrift. *A. plantaginea* 'Bees' Ruby' is a good plant for the front of a border, with bright rose-pink globe-like heads borne on 38 to 45 cm (15 to 18 in) stems from June until August. The forms of *A. maritima*, sea thrift, are dwarfs but are also long-flowering, making good edging plants as well as being useful in a ribbon border of strong-growing alpines. Set 30 cm (12 in) apart.

Artemisia absinthium 'Lambrook Silver'. One of the finest foliage plants for the border, it is useful throughout the summer when its finely cut, silver-white leaves act as a foil to more brightly coloured subjects. It reaches a height of 90 cm (3 ft). Set 60 cm (2 ft) apart.

Aruncus. For moist soils in shade, the old *Spiraea aruncus* is invaluable. In these conditions the 2 m (about 6 ft) creamy-white flower plumes will last over several weeks and the plant will remain well clothed in foliage. One plant will adequately fill a square metre (a square yard or more).

Aster. The Michaelmas daisies, as a group, suffer from mildew and need staking excepting for the 'dwarf' varieties (15 to 30 cm (6 to 12 in)). However, their flowers are so soon over that they do not answer the purpose of the weekend gardener for whom it is more satisfactory to concentrate on dwarf bedding-dahlias and the more compact-growing hardy bush chrysanthemums which will provide autumn colour in the flower border. The only member of the genus worth the weekend gardener's space is the August-October blooming *A.* × *frikartii*.

Astilbe. This is a beautiful subject for moist rich soil. It is referred to in Chapter Three as it is an ideal weed-suppressor for moist soil. Any good catalogue of perennials lists an assortment of varieties in colours varying from white through pale pink and lilac, to rose and crimson. Most should be set at about 60 cm (2 ft) apart.

Bergenia. Again this will be found in Chapter Three. Flowering in very early spring, its main asset for the flower border is its fleshy paddle-shaped leaves which are effective at the front of taller plants.

Bupthalmum. A trouble-free plant which blooms over a long period, usually from June to August, *Bupthalmum salicifolium* carries an abundance of deep-yellow, small 'daisies' on short, stout stems up to 60 cm (2 ft) high. Set 60 cm (2 ft) apart.

Campanula. In this family, one of the best species for the absent gardener's purpose is the white-suffused violet-flowered *C.* × *burghaltii* with its drooping, satiny bells on stems about 30 to 45 cm (12 to 18 in) high. Flowering in June and July, if the spent spikes are removed it will often bloom again in autumn. 'Pouffe' is a dwarf hybrid of *C. lactiflora*, that covers itself with harebell blue-to-mauve flowers over a long spell in summer and is useful at the front of the border. Also good is the purple *C. glomerata* 'Superba' which reaches about 75 cm (2½ ft) in height. Set about 60 cm (2 ft) apart. Unfortunately the pretty, pale-blue or white *C. lactiflora* itself needs the dead bells constantly picking off if it is not to look unsightly, and it may need to be staked in windy weather.

Centranthus. The valerian makes a long-lasting show of crimson, pink or white flower-heads, reaching a height of 60 to 90 cm (2 to 3 ft) from May to August. Self-sown seedlings occur but these can easily be pulled up if they are not wanted. It will grow almost anywhere, and is a most valuable and colourful plant. Needing no care, it is an ideal subject for the weekend gardener.

Chrysanthemum. Many people like to grow a clump or two of the white *C. maximum*. The semi-double and double sorts cannot be called trouble-free, but sturdy, single whites such as 'Everest' more or less look after themselves. The only support needed is a circular plant hoop which soon becomes inconspicuous in the border. Alternatively they can be grown towards the front and allowed to 'flop'. Plants should be divided every two or three years. *C. rubellum* flowers in late summer and autumn reaching about 60 cm (2 ft) in height. In some gardens it will go on for several years, but in others it needs constant renewal from cuttings—not always an easy matter for the weekend gardener to arrange. 'Clara Curtis' (pink), 'Duchess of Edinburgh' (red) and 'Mary Stokes' (yellow) are among the varieties readily obtainable. Best for most gardens are the dwarf varieties of the Korean chrysanthemum, or the pompon sorts.

C. roseum (syn. *C. coccineum*), the pyrethrum, is an early-summer flowerer but it is not among the most trouble-free of garden plants. Main requirements are a rich well-drained soil and an open position. Given these it will succeed over much of the south, but in the damper north and west is apt to succumb in winter. The single-flowered sorts are a better bet than the doubles in colder, damper areas. They need some support if they are not to look untidy, but this can easily be arranged by surrounding the clumps with short pea-sticks which will quickly be disguised by the carroty foliage.

Coreopsis verticillata. An excellent plant for the weekend gardener, flowering as it does from June to August and needing no staking. It will not grow on poor, dry soils but elsewhere it is a reliable plant, forming shapely domes of deep green covered with starry, yellow flowers and reaching a height of about 45 cm (18 in).

Curtonus paniculatus. This is similar to an extra strong crocosmia but not so free-flowering. *C. paniculatus* 'Major' is the best form to choose and is quite hardy.

Cynara cardunculus (see also Chapter Three). A massively architectural plant with a very long season of interest. It is similar to the globe artichoke to which family it belongs, and it makes a handsome border addition.

Dictamnus albus (syn. *fraxinella*). A good front- or middle-row plant with snowy-white flowers that will grow in almost any soil so long as it is well drained and in a sunny position. *D. a. purpureus* has showy spikes of rosy-lilac. Three plants should be set about 45 cm (18 in) apart for the best effect.

Digitalis. The foxglove is a biennial but several strains, such as 'Excelsior', will sow themselves and naturalize in the border. Some also survive over a number of years. They are so attractive, easy, and trouble-free that it is well worth devoting a patch to them.

Doronicum. The leopard's bane is an early yellow 'daisy' with a long season of flower. The hybrid 'Miss Mason' starts to flower in April quite near to the ground and continues into May, when it reaches a height of about 45 cm (18 in). Flowering for a period of from six to eight weeks and making sturdy, compact clumps, it is a worthwhile subject to replace the daffodils which are troublesome to grow in the flower border on account of the unsightliness of their withering leaves.

The later *D. pardalianches* 'Golden Bunch' is rather taller and flowers from May to July, its rich yellow 'daisies' borne four or five to a stem.

Echinops. The globe thistles are valuable border plants for later summer. Most remain in beauty for several weeks in July and August. All are deep-rooted and reliably perennial with long, greyish, somewhat prickly leaves and handsome globular heads on stiff stems. They are as decorative for cutting as they are in the garden. The best for general planting, reaching to 90 cm (3 ft) or more but needing no staking, is *E. ritro*. The form of this species known as 'Veitch's Blue' is worth looking out for. It has glaucous silver foliage and bright-blue flower-heads.

Eremurus. Strictly for dry, sunny places, the eremurus should be tried. These fox-tail lilies are magnificent border subjects producing dense, long-lasting spikes of flower on stems up to almost 2·5 m (8 ft) tall and ranging in colour from pure white to pink, gold, amber, orange and copper. They must have perfect drainage, full sun, wind shelter, good loam and low rainfall but if your garden measures up to these requirements they are plants you should not miss. They seldom succeed in cold or excessively damp areas. Their fleshy roots radiate in starfish form from a central crown and are very brittle, so great care must be exercised in planting. The crown should be set 8 or 10 cm (3 or 4 in) below the surface with the centre on a little mound of sand and the tuberous roots radiating outwards and downwards. A broad hole is needed as the root-spread of some species may be up to over 80 cm (32 in) in diameter. When the clumps achieve more than four flowering spikes they must be raised and divided. The late Sir Frederick Stern, who was one of the great authorities on the genus, advised that the clumps be raised by two men inserting forks on either side and slowly lifting the plant which should then be put into a cool, dry shed. Once the soil on the roots has dried it becomes easy to divide the clump into several flowering plants. The best for general purposes are the Shelford hybrids and the Highdown hybrids (raised by Sir Frederick Stern himself). As the stems are so tall the plants look more pleasing if emerging from behind a screen of foliage. At Bodnant the autumn-flowering *Erica stricta* is used and grown to a height of about 90 cm (3 ft) to form a kind of knot-bed in which eremurus and *Lilium auratum* are grown. In the garden of his country cottage in Berkshire, my brother-in-law, Professor Dan Lewis, who holds the Chair of Botany at University College, London, grows his eremurus in association with fennel, the feathery foliage of which forms an ideal, sheltering screen for the eremurus stems.

Eryngium. The sea holly is rather similar in some ways to the globe thistle but is often even bluer and much more handsome, with silvery leaves. Unfortunately, most need sunny, well-drained positions. One of the best is *E. amethystinum* with jagged green leaves and amethyst-blue heads from July to September. It reaches about 75 cm (2½ ft). *E. alpinum* is also good, with deeply jagged leaves and silvery-blue flower heads. Of the two similar genera, the echinops are more accommodating as to soil and climate than the eryngiums, but the latter are smaller, more attractive, and therefore more suitable for modest borders.

Euphorbia. Apart from the well-known and statuesque *E. wulfenii* of spring (see Chapter Three) which is definitely shrubby in character, *E. nicaeensis* is a good weekend gardener's plant, with narrow glaucous leaves and carrying exotic-looking lime-green flowers for almost three months from late May until mid-August. Reaching a height of 45 cm (18 in), it needs no staking and is at its best in poor, dry soil in sun. It may be obtained from Unusual Plants, White Barn House, Elmstead Market, Near Colchester, Essex.

Filipendula, (formerly spiraea). The meadowsweets are satisfactory in any soil which does not dry out in summer although, like the astilbes, they are at their best in moist places. The double form of the native meadowsweet, *F. hexapetala* is not at all fussy about soil or moisture and will grow well even in dry soil in sun. The creamy-white heads are carried on 45 to 50 cm (18 to 20 in) stems in June and July above the dark green dense, ferny foliage. *F. purpurea* is even more pleasing but does need a rich, moist soil and some shade. It carries heads of carmine-red flowers in July, but really does not remain in bloom long enough for the weekender's garden. *F. rubra,* on the other hand, goes on blooming intermittently over a long period. It needs no staking if grown in the kind of sheltered, moist place it enjoys best, although its deep-rose flowers are carried on 120 cm (4 ft) stems.

Geranium. (see also Chapter Three). Of the hardy species of meadow cranesbill, *G. pratense* makes a good border plant, especially in the double forms which remain in bloom for three weeks or more. *G. p.* 'Plenum Caeruleum' is the best colour form with double clear-blue flowers. There is also a purple-blue form and a double white which is unfortunately now exceedingly rare. *G. grandiflorum* 'Alpinum' is a fine front-row plant, making wide mats (90 cm (3 ft) of dense, pretty foliage covered with large, clear-blue salver-like flowers.

Helenium. Of this popular border plant, only the shorter varieties can be recommended to the absent gardener on account of the staking problem. Best of these are the bright-yellow 'Crimson Beauty', and 'Wyndley' (coppery orange). They flower for a period of six to eight weeks and occupy a space of about 60 by 60 cm (2 ft square).

Heliopsis. This genus is among the best of the 'daisies'. Its varieties come in various shades of yellow and flower from July to September. 'Summer Sun' is one of the best for our purpose with orange-yellow flowers borne on strong, branching stems at a height of 90 cm (3 ft). This is one of those plants which a hoop support might help in windy areas. Otherwise the only care needed is the occasional removal of faded flowers which detract from the appearance of the clump.

Hemerocallis. Although the individual flowers of the day lilies last for only one day, there is a continuous succession of blooms, and the period of flowering covers many weeks from mid-summer on. Their clumps of strap-shaped leaves make good weed-suppressors. The plants are long-lived, will grow in any soil, wet or dry, in sun or partial shade, although they will not do quite as well in poor, parched soil as in the deep, rich soil they prefer. Like many others they pay for good treatment in the form of a bucketful of compost or moist peat incorporated at planting time. Many varieties are now available, of which some of the best are the apricot-orange 'Desert Song'; 'George Yeld' (tawny orange); 'Hiawatha' (coppery); 'Hyperion' (a very fine canary yellow); 'Margaret Perry' (tangerine-orange); 'Marie Ballard' (salmon-apricot); 'Saladin' (bronzy-crimson) and 'Pink Charm' which is the nearest approach to pink. In the border they are useful to cover the dying foliage of daffodils and tulips—a function which they share with the large-leafed hostas and the agapanthus.

Heuchera (see Chapter Three).

Hosta (see also Chapter Three). Fine front-row, foliage plants for the border or for ground cover. Mainly grown for the attraction of their leaves, the lavender-coloured lily-like spires of flower in June and July are an added bonus.

Inula. In its best forms this is a choice border perennial, easy and trouble-free, with yellow daisy-like flowers. Some, however, are too tall and others only briefly in flower or tending to dry out. The longest blooming, self-supporting and most generally satisfactory varieties are *I. ensifolia* 'Compacta' which makes a neat 30 cm (12 in) high mound covered with golden 'daisies' for many weeks from July to September, and 'Golden Beauty' which is similar but taller at 60 cm (2 ft).

Kniphofia. The red-hot pokers will withstand drought and neglect but must have sharp drainage and full sun. In cold, wet districts the leaves should be tied together at the onset of winter to protect the crowns. Among the most reliable are *K. caulescens*, with broad blue-grey leaves and 1·2 m (4 ft) spikes of a salmon-rose colour fading to cream, which forms sturdy clumps as much as 1·2 m (4 ft) across; the daintier *K. galpinii* which needs a light, well-drained soil in a mild area and carries its orange-flame pokers on 60 cm (2 ft) stems above narrow, grass-like leaves; 'Bees' Lemon' which reaches 90 cm (3 ft); the ivory-blush 'Maid of Orleans'—90 cm (3 ft) high and across; and the well-known red and yellow 'Royal Standard' which grows to 1·2 m (4 ft). On chalk, where they do particularly well, they make good weed-suppressing subjects.

Ligularia. This is one of the best perennials for damp places, having huge, handsome leaves and sprays of yellow or orange 'daisies'. The best varieties are 'Gregynog Gold', and *L. dentata* 'Desdemona' which has orange flowers and purplish leaves. When established they flower for several weeks from July, making large clumps with 60 to 90 cm (2 to 3 ft) stems and a 90 cm (3 ft) spread.

Linum narbonense. An attractive front-of-the-border plant, flax needs well-drained soil. Given this, it is hardy, trouble-free and long-lived. Its clouds of soft, bright-blue flowers are delightful from June till September and are borne on wiry stems needing no support. The best form is 'Heavenly Blue'.

Mimulus luteus. A showy plant for damp places, reaching a height of 45 cm (18 in). The type has bright-yellow flowers and there is a form 'A. T. Johnson' with particularly showy mahogany-and-yellow blooms.

Monarda didyma. One of the most florally effective of the herbs, the bergamot carries whorls of honeysuckle-type flowers in scarlet, pink or purple on 90 cm (3 ft) stems over a long period from June onwards. The plants need good soil and some moisture, otherwise they tend to die out. If they have a fault it is the tendency to make matted growth, necessitating the detaching and replanting of tufts of the outer growth at 15 to 23 cm (6 to 9 in) apart. This operation should be carried out in March, as if it is done in autumn the plants may be lost through winter damp. Alternatively, mulching the clumps with good loamy soil laced with leaf mould should stimulate the centres to new growth.

The well-known 'Cambridge Scarlet' has now been replaced by the better, modern, 'Adam'. Other good varieties are 'Croftway Pink', 'Melissa' (also pink but with larger flowers), 'Pillar Box' (scarlet), 'Prairie Glow' (salmon-red), and 'Prairie Night' (magenta-purple).

Nepeta. *N. faassenii*, the catmint, is a good plant for an open sunny spot where it will make a mist of lavender blue for several weeks in summer. It should be cut hard back after flowering to promote new basal growth. 'Six Hills Giant' is a fine cultivar, but 'Souvenir d'André Chaudron' is even better and more upstanding with 60 cm (2 ft) flower spikes from June to August. Its vigorous root-spread may well be an asset to the absent gardener as it tends to take care of vacant ground between plants.

Oenothera. Of the evening primroses, the longest-flowering period comes from the *fruticosa* varieties which grow to 45 cm (18 in) or so and are set with bright yellow flowers about 5 cm (2 in) across from June to August. Of these, the finest is probably 'Yellow River'. More fussy as to soil, which should be sharply drained and in full sun, is the beautiful *O. missouriensis* which needs a front-of-the-border position as it tends to sprawl. Its larger flowers—up to 10 cm (4 in) across—are lemon yellow and open from pointed red buds. It flowers throughout July and August and often into September.

Omphalodes cappadocica. A charming spring-flowering plant, this has 15 cm (6 in) sprays of bright blue flowers from April to June. It often flowers again during the autumn.

Paeonia. The paeonies, though beautiful, do not have a long flowering period. Moreover, the taller Chinese forms need staking, but this can easily be catered for by the provision of ring plant-supports in spring. A selection, including the well-known cottage doubles in crimson and pink and some of the Chinese sorts, can be arranged to give a long season of interest. The fragrant, crimson-tipped, white 'Festiva Maxima', the cherry-crimson 'Cherry Hill', and the silver-rose 'Edulis Superba' are early to bloom and these could well be followed by the carmine-centred, pink 'Albert Crousse', the carmine 'Felix Crousse' and the wine-red 'Karl Rosenfield'.

Penstemon. For milder counties, given full sun and sharp drainage, the penstemons are excellent border plants. One of the best, the pink *P. campanulatus* 'Evelyn' sends up 60 cm (2 ft) spikes from July to September. *P. gentianoides* 'Alice Hindley', taller with large, lavender-blue foxglove-like flowers, grows up to 1·2 m (4 ft). *P. campanulatus* 'Garnet', taller than 'Evelyn', reaches nearly 90 cm (3 ft), with wine-red trumpets. There are also the bedding hybrids, some of which may prove perennial, but most of which will probably need to be renewed every year.

Perovskia (see also p. 71). This is really a shrub, but nevertheless makes a fine border plant for a sunny spot. It appreciates good soil but should not be planted in a damp ground or in clay.

Phygelius capensis, Cape figwort. For all but the coldest areas and soils this is a good border plant, making strong branching stems up to 1·2 cm (4 ft) and needing no staking. The bright scarlet flowers are borne from July until October.

Physostegia speciosa, the obedient plant. A genus of fairly long-blooming, medium-height plants, reaching 60 to 75 cm (2 to 2½ ft) in height, with shapely spikes of conspicuous tubular, lipped flowers. 'Rose Bouquet' has rose-pink blooms from early August to the end of

September. *P. virginiana* tends to be taller and should be planted in poor, sharply drained soil or it may 'flop'. The best varieties are the lilac 'Summer Spire' and white 'Summer Snow'. Both these flower through July and August.

Platycodon grandiflorus, balloon flower. *P. g.* 'Mariesii' is the best for our purpose. Being dwarf it can be grown without staking and its violet-blue balloons open to shapely cupped blossoms 5 cm (2 in) or more across. Even if the stems sprawl. the blossoms still face upwards merely giving the effect of a larger clump. The species is accommodating as to soil, and *P.* '*Mariesii*' will often bloom from July to September. There is a white form *P. g.* 'Album' which is also good. All the other cultivars are taller and must be staked; neither do they last long in flower.

Polygonum amplexicaule 'Atrosanguineum' is a showy tall plant that needs no staking, although reaching to a height of 1·2 cm (4 ft). From July to October it carries bright-red spikes of wiry little bottle brushes above a dark-green-foliaged, bushy clump. It is accommodating as to soil but prefers sun to shade and will grow taller in more moist conditions.

Primula. Apart from the primrose and polyanthus primrose, the genus contains many other useful plants, including the attractive *P. denticulata*, the drumstick primula, which bears globular heads of lavender, purple or white from March to May. At its best in strong, moist soil, it is nevertheless reasonably accommodating and may always be helped by just a scattering of wood ash or bonemeal. Various named sorts may be found in the catalogues. Two of the best are 'Taylor's Violet' and 'Crimson Emperor'. Later to bloom, the Asiatic candelabra primulas, although often referred to as bog primulas, will do well in good deep garden soil that has enough humus to retain moisture, reaching a height of 45 to 60 cm (18 to 24 in). *P. japonica* (white, pink, red); *bulleyana* (apricot); *helodoxa* (yellow) and *pulverulenta* (shades of pink) give a magnificent show in June and July. The later-blooming, giant cowslip-flowered types, *sikkimensis* and *florindae*, are pale yellow and very sweetly scented. *P. sikkimensis* grows to 60 cm (2 ft) while *florindae* is taller at 90 cm (3 ft) or more.

Pyrethrum, see *Chrysanthemum roseum*.

Scabiosa caucasica. One of the most popular border plants. It does not need staking and is very long-flowering. If it has a fault it is that the plants tend to deteriorate or even die out after three or four years and should be replaced by yearling plants. Light, rather than heavy, friable soil on the alkaline side of neutral suits them best, and they should always be planted in spring. As to varieties, the well-known

'Clive Greaves' has never been surpassed and has a good constitution. 'Penhill Blue' is also good, while the creamy-white 'Miss Willmott' makes an interesting contrast.

Sedum (see also Chapter Three). The *spectabile* and *maximum* forms are as suitable for the border as for ground cover and have the virtue of being virtually self-maintaining.

Sidalcea. This is a genus that looks rather weedy to me, but many people like it and the plants flower over many weeks and are virtually trouble-free. The best are the bushy 'Croftway Red'—90 cm (3 ft); the compact 'Dainty', white-eyed, rose-pink; and the shell-pink 'Loveliness'—60 cm (2 ft).

Stachys. *S. lanata*, lamb's ears, has been dealt with in Chapter Three. Here, I would like to recommend *S. macrantha* 'Superba' (formerly *Betonica grandiflora*) which makes sturdy 60 cm (2 ft) bushes topped with plump spikes of showy lilac-rose flowers in June and July. This is a fine front-row plant for the border or it may be used to very good effect to underplant most roses. It is delightful also beneath the white 'Iceberg' floribunda rose, when grown as a shrub or in a bed on its own.

Stokesia laevis. This is the best of the 'cornflowers'. The large, lavender-blue flowers are borne on 30 cm (12 in) stems that are well set with leathery dark-green, long leaves. It does well in any soil.

Thalictrum. The meadow rues are so outstandingly lovely as to make their faults seem all the more regrettable. One variety that needs no staking is the May-to-June-flowering *T. aquilegifolium* 'Bees' Purple' which carries clouds of tiny, rose-purple flowers on 90 cm (3 ft) stems. It needs a reasonably good, deep soil, but is not fussy as to sun or shade. The outstanding *T. dipterocarpum* has a poor constitution and its mauve, yellow-centred flowerlets are borne on such tall, slender stems that it has to be staked, which at $1\frac{1}{2}$ to 2 m (5 to 6 ft) is a problem. *T. flavum* is easier with pretty, deep-green, glossy foliage and heads of citron-yellow fluffy flowers. The stems of this species are stronger but the flowering period is rather brief. However, the form *T. glaucum* has such attractive blue-grey foliage that the plant is pleasing all summer, and its flowers are of a particular soft and pleasant yellow. *T. minus*, the hardy maidenhair, is grown purely for its foliage which is reminiscent of that of a maidenhair fern and good for cutting. It grows to about 75 cm ($2\frac{1}{2}$ ft).

Tradescantia. The genus includes some of the longest-flowering border plants. They are easy, trouble-free and will grow almost anywhere and in any type of soil. All have grass-like foliage and clustered heads of three-petalled flowers. The best varieties are 'Iris Pritchard' (white with blue centre), 'Isis' (Oxford blue), and 'Leonora' (mid-blue). It reaches 30 cm (1 ft) in height with a 60 cm (2 ft) spread.

Trollius. The globe flower needs a deep, moist soil where it can make compact clumps with striking ball-shaped flowers over several weeks in spring. The best varieties are 'Alabaster' (ivory-primrose), 'Canary Bird' (lemon), 'Prichard's Giant' (gold), and 'Orange Princess'. They grow to about 75 cm (2½ ft) in height with a comparable spread, and flower in May and June.

Verbena. For mild areas and sunny, dry borders the dwarf *V. corymbosa* makes a good front-row bushy plant with clustered heads of heliotrope flowers from July to September. It is particularly effective grown on a bank or on top of an earth-filled wall.

Veronica. *V. longifolia* is the longest-flowering member of the family, bearing blue, pink, or white spikes, according to variety, on 90 cm (3 ft) stems from July to September. One of the best forms is *V. l. subsessilis (hendersonii)*. *V. spicata* is earlier to flower and blooms for about two weeks. Both species need good soil and *spicata* should be divided and replanted every two or three years. Reaching to about 60 cm (2 ft) in height, the best forms of the latter are 'Blue Spire', the pink 'Barcarolle', and 'Romily Purple'.

ANNUALS AND BIENNIALS

Few annuals are worth the weekend gardener's attention as most either require too much attention during the early seedling stage or need the provision of twiggy supports which are unsightly until the plants have grown. Exceptions are *Iberis amara*, the annual candytuft, which forms well-branched, sturdy, self-supporting little plants with heads of pink, mauve, red and purple; *Linaria* 'Giant Bouquet', the fairy flax; and *Limnanthes douglasii*, the appealing eggs-and-bacon plant, which will often seed itself for several years and is delightful if grown in yellow and white drifts at the forefront of shrubs. We grow mysotis, forget-me-not, on the same principle, pulling up the plants before mildew can strike in the summer but shaking out the seeds among the shrubs before consigning the remains to the compost heap. Flower arrangers may also like to try *Helichrysum bracteatum* 'Monstrosum', an everlasting which is as useful for drying off as for garden display and comes in colours of orange-red, terracotta, gold, yellow, and white. For indoor decoration the flowers should be cut as soon as they have fully opened. They should then be bunched and hung head down in a cool, airy place to dry out completely. Properly prepared like this they will last over many dark winter months. Lunaria, honesty, is a biennial that seeds itself freely. If the lavender- or white-flowered strains are sown, it can be a pleasant garden addition.

BULBS

For the weekend gardener as for others, much of the pleasure of a garden comes from bulbs. Taking up little space, if grown in the border their dying foliage may be disguised by that of other plants. Even the problem of the fading daffodil leaves can be offset by growing the bulbs among plants with vigorous foliage. We grow ours among paeonies (the scarlet snout and bronze young leaves help to set off the daffodil flowers), day lilies and hostas, where the withering foliage is barely noticeable. Some people sow the annual blue convolvulus, *Convolvulus tricolor* 'Blue Ensign' and other cultivars, among the daffodils, leaving the bushy growth of the annuals to cover the withering leaves—or one can plant one's daffodils in grass which need not be cut until after the foliage has withered. For the over-gardened weekender who has to concentrate his efforts into the area surrounding the house and leave the remainder of the garden to flowering or fruiting trees set in grass, this can be most rewarding. Paths are cut through the sweeps of grass with a rotor mower and the rest left as a flowery meadow until late June. A second cutting in September will clear the way for the colchicums to come through in autumn.

Anemone. Many people have difficulty in flowering the florist's large De Caen and St Brigid anemones. This may be overcome by soaking the corms in water for twenty-four hours before planting. These types need a sunny, well-drained spot if they are to last more than a season or two. More likely to naturalize are the blue, pink, mauve and white daisy-flowered, early *A. blanda* and *A. appenina* which follows in April. Of these two species, *A. blanda* succeeds best in the south and has in fact become a beautiful weed, seeding itself right through the shrub belts in some places. It is particularly good on chalk and can be seen naturalized in the late Sir Frederick Stern's garden at Highdown, near Worthing, in Sussex. With us in North Wales, it was only *A. appenina* that behaved like this, making a welcome and lovely carpet to set off our dwarf rhododendron and azalea species. In the north and west, *A. blanda* does best on sharply drained terrace beds or among rocks. In my view the blue flowers are by far the loveliest.

Camassia. The weekend gardener with rough grass to beautify might plant some of the camassia species. They thrive on almost any soil but will not flower in heavy shade. Quite hardy, they do well even on cold clays, often naturalizing themselves. Bearing tall spikes clothed for the top few inches in starry blue or white flowers, all are good. The finest, the pale blue *C. cusickii*, is not always obtainable, but *C. leichtlinii* with flowers of deeper blue or white, and *C. quamash* (sometimes listed as *C. esculenta*), the Canadian bear grass with tall, pale blue starry spires, are pleasing. The large bulbs should be planted about 8 cm (3 in) deep and apart.

Chionodoxa. Like all early bulbs, the chionodoxas last in flower over several weeks. All are good, the deep blue *C. gigantea* and its form 'Alba' having the largest blooms, but *C. luciliae* is lovely and prolific, often increasing by seed and offsets, with paler blue white-eyed flowers. Set 2·5 cm (1 in) deep and 8 cm (3 in) apart.

Colchicum. Like the camassia, these should be confined to rough grass on account of their large, strap-like leaves which appear in spring. The bulbs flower in autumn (they are popularly known as autumn crocuses), producing quantities of large crocus-like chalices. All are good, often lasting in bloom for almost two months. Set 13 cm (5 in) deep and 10 cm (4 in) apart.

Crocus. It is the early species crocus which are the best value as they seed freely and bloom over a long period. The two best species for general planting are *C. tomasinianus* and its hybrids (lavender) and *C. chrysanthus* and its seedlings which vary in colour from white, violet-shaded on the outside of the cup, to a real blue, buttercup yellow, primrose, and yellow striped with bronze. They are ideal to plant at the front of sunny beds or in grass which need not be trimmed until after the leaves have withered. Set 5 cm (2 in) deep and apart.

Corms set in the open ground are subject to the depredations of mice but this can be guarded against by surrounding the plantings with barricades of spiny gorse shoots. It is worth noting that crocuses planted in grass or among carpeting ivy, aubrieta or periwinkle will seldom be taken by mice. In addition to the spring kinds mentioned, it is worth planting the true autumn crocus, *C. speciosus*, among deciduous azaleas or to surround a Japanese maple because the pure blue-lavender of the cups is so splendidly set off by the scarlet autumn leaves.

Cyclamen, The hardy dwarf cyclamen are delightful and easy if established from growing corms that can usually be obtained from alpine specialists or from such firms as Broadleigh Gardens, Barr House, Bishops Hull, Taunton, Somerset, TA4 1AE. Most flower over a fairly long period and in the case of *C. neapolitanum* the beautifully silvered, ivy-shaped leaves are an additional long-lasting asset. *C. orbiculatum* and *C.o. coum* are also worth growing if you are able to visit your weekend retreat during the winter months. Their small shubby 'shuttlecocks' in pink, crimson, or white, rise above the dark green, rounded leaves from Christmas on, and are particularly effective companions to the bright-blue *Iris histrioides*, early snowdrops such as *Galanthus elwesii*, and eranthis, winter aconite. It is important to note that while *Cyclamen neaoplitanum* roots from the top, *C. orbiculatum* roots from below, so if planting dried corms one should always look for traces of dried-off roots and be sure to get the corms the right way up.

Daffodil see *Narcissus*.

Endymion hispanicus, the tall Spanish bluebell, makes a show for several weeks in May and early June and is particularly useful among shrubs. There are blue, white and pink forms, but the pink tends to be rather muddy in colour.

Eranthis, winter aconite. This is one of those maddening subjects which will grow well in some gardens, spreading over a wide area, but in others gradually die out. Where it does well it is a delight, so it is worth trying a few bulbs and seeing what happens. It prefers a not too moist, woodsy soil, and should be set about 5 cm (2 in) apart and deep. Apart from *E. hyemalis*, flowering early in January, there is *E. cilicica* with deeper yellow flowers and bronzy foliage and the later, much larger, flowered hybrid *E.* × *tubergenii* 'Glory' and 'Guinea Gold'.

Erythronium. In addition to the early dog's-tooth violet, *E. dens-canis*, the taller, creamy *E. californicum* and the rose-pink *E. revolutum* should also be planted. Over the years, in a partly shaded, leafy soil, they will naturalize themselves, making an extremely pretty carpet beneath shrubs or trees. They do not like too dry a spot. Set about 10 cm (4 in) deep and 5 cm (2 in) apart.

Fritillaria. The weekend gardener might like to try *F. imperialis*, the crown imperial, which is a spectacular companion for the doronicums in the spring border, growing 90 cm (3 ft) tall with hanging crowns of orange or lemon bells beneath showy tufts of dark green leaves. The crown imperials need good, well-drained loam, preferably limy, and full sun, and should be set 20 cm (8 in) deep and apart. *F. meleagris* 'Alba' is also worth planting for its drooping white bells that look like fairy lanterns in the illustrations for a children's story and are most attractive among shrubs or in grass. They appreciate a moist soil and grow wild in damp meadows in Oxfordshire and Suffolk where the chequered snake's-head form is usually seen.

Galanthus, snowdrop. Most people who visit their garden during the winter months like to be greeted by drifts of snowdrops, and in most parts of Britain the common *G. nivalis* is easy to grow, provided it is planted 'in the green'—as a growing bulb just after the flowers have faded. If you cannot arrange this, then it pays to plant the dry bulbs in September, allow them to flower, and dig them up and replant them again in their permanent positions once the flowers have faded. Apart from *G. nivalis* which grows well in grass or among shrubs and prefers a well-drained loam and a dressing of leaf-mould, the earlier, giant snowdrop, *G. elwesii* is worth growing and should be given a sunny spot in well-drained soil. The more sun it receives during its summer resting period, the earlier and better it will flower. All snowdrops benefit from a dressing of bonemeal annually. They should be set 5 to 8 cm (2 to 3 in) deep and 5 cm (2 in) apart.

Galtonia, Cape hyacinth. An easy and cheap, lily-like bulb to grace the border in summer. *G. candicans* has ivory-white hanging bells of a solid texture, spaced for 25 cm (10 in) or more along the 90 to 120 cm (3 to 4 ft) stems. It should be set in spring 13 cm (5 in) deep and 15 cm (6 in) apart. Flower arrangers might like to grow also the green-belled *G. princeps*.

Hermodactylus tuberosus. This flowers in March and April and is worth growing for its velvety, black and green iris-like flowers. From 23 to 25 cm (9 to 10 in) tall, it should be set in reasonably good but well-drained soil 8 cm (3 in) deep and 5 cm (2in) apart.

Hyacinth. Long-lasting but very formal in appearance, the hyacinths mainly have their place in tubs, window-boxes or bowls for the house.

Iris. If you have a spot in poor soil near a south-facing wall or on a south-facing rock bank, *Iris unguicularis* (the erstwhile *stylosa*) will give you weekends of pleasure, coming into bloom whenever the weather is frost-free from November until March. Clumps take three years to flower, after which they will go on for ever. The only problem is that of slug damage and these pests should be tackled at the beginning of November to ensure quantities of the large, fragrant, delicate-looking lavender-and-white blooms that unroll from tightly furled fawn, umbrella-like buds. *I. histrioides* and *I. reticulata*, flowering in January and February respectively, are well worth growing in any sunny, raised spot, either alone or in association with other early-flowering bulbs. They range in colour from piercing bright blue to Cambridge blue and purple, and *reticulata* has a delightful, pervading, violet fragrance. Set 5 cm (2 in) deep and apart.

The Dutch irises suffer from an individually short flowering period but one or two groups towards the front of the border help to prolong the colour once the daffodils are over. Like the daffodils, their dying leaves can be a problem but if they are set among paeonies, hellebores, hostas and other plants with prolific foliage, their decay will go almost unnoticed. Even more useful, and certainly more permanent, are the English irises which bloom in July and are helpful to fill gaps in the continuity of flowering. Set 15 cm (6 in) deep and apart.

Leucojum. Both the February-to-March-flowering snowflake, *Leuco-jum vernum*, and the inexactly named summer snowflake, *L. aestivum* which blooms from April to May, are worth a place. *L. vernum* likes a sunny position in well-drained soil where it will increase to form size-able clumps of substantially petalled little flowers with hanging heads tipped with green—for all the world like lampshades of the 1920s. *L. aestivum* 'Gravetye Giant' carries several swinging bells on stems up to 45 cm (18 in) or more tall. Both should be set 8 cm (3 in) apart and deep

Muscari, grape hyacinth. Complaints may be registered about the 'grass' of the useful *Muscari armeniacum* 'Heavenly Blue' but it is such an attractive bulb with its thimbles of colourful flowers that I think it should be forgiven. It may be ribbon planted at the forefront of shrubs and borders or grown in grass where its foliage may not be noticed. *M. a.* 'Cantab' with Cambridge-blue flowers and the white *M. botryoides* 'Album' may also be planted and should be set about 5 cm (2 in) apart and deep.

Narcissus. The best 'daffodils' for naturalizing in grass are the vigorous 'doers' that are free-flowering and prolific in increase such as 'Carlton', 'Flower Carpet', the apricot-frilled 'John Evelyn', the white 'Mount Hood' and *N. poeticus*, the old fragrant pheasant's-eye narcissus. For selected places in borders or among shrubs where nearby plantings of hostas, hellebores, ferns or day lilies can disguise their fading foliage, good modern varieties to choose are the white 'Broughshane', golden 'Kingscourt', or 'Hunter's Moon' among the large trumpets. 'Fore-sight' with a white perianth and lemon corona is early and refreshing. Also good are 'Spellbinder', a reversed bi-colour in greeny-sulphur-lemon of which the inside of the trumpet in a few days turns to white; 'Armada' a sun-proof, large-cupped variety with golden perianth and and frilled cup of bright, deep tangerine; 'Ceylon' which is also sun-proof; 'Kilworth' a small-cupped red-and-white flower with vivid orange-red cup; 'Ludlow' a large-cupped white with greenish base to the crown; the pink 'Rose of Tralee' and 'Louise de Coligny'; 'Limerick', with flat cherry-red cup and white perianth; 'Bryher' with white cup and perianth—the only hint of colour being a touch of emerald green in the centre; the Tazetta group such as 'Geranium' and the creamy, double, several-flowered 'Cheerfulness'.

Taking up little space, and with much less conspicuous foliage, are dwarf hybrids such as the early 'February Gold', 'March Sunshine', 'Peeping Tom' with its characteristically long golden trumpet, the white 'Jenny' and the white and primrose 'Dove Wings.' These are all *cyclamineus* hybrids reaching from 20 to 25 cm (8 to 10 in) in height.

Later follow the *triandrus* hybrids—'Liberty Bells' with two to four gracefully hanging flowers of lemon yellow, the glistening white 'Rippling Waters' with three or four reflexed perianth flowers per stem and 'Silver Chimes' which may have up to a dozen flowers of the *N. triandrus* type dropping from a 25 cm (10 in) stem. There is also the 15 cm (6 in) 'Beryl' with its beautifully shaped lemon-yellow perianth and small bright orange cup. Apart from these, if you have a damp place in grass or at the edge of a stream, which is in sunshine and tends to become drier in summer, you can try the February-blooming *N. cyclamineus* itself which carries on 10 cm (4 in) stems long slender golden trumpets with sharply reflexed perianths. The wild hoop-petticoat narcissus from Spain—*N. bulbocodium*—requires a slightly drier position and succeeds best with a little sand in the soil.

Nerine. For a place in the 'eye of the sun' as the saying is, these beautiful South African flowers cannot be beaten. They flower in autumn and when established will give a succession of bloom over several weeks from late September often until frost. Given sun and a well-drained soil they are hardy as far north as Perthshire. Their handsome, strap-shaped leaves are no trouble and die inconspicuously away just before the flower stems appear. Glistening-pink, crinkly petalled flowers are borne in whorled heads on 30 to 45 cm (12 to 18 in) stems. The bulbs should be planted 2½ cm (1 in) or more deep in March. When, at last, they become overcrowded they should be divided in the same month.

Oxalis. The common little *O. floribunda* is a cheerful and bright plant for the foreground of shrubs or border or to inhabit a ribbon border of tougher alpines. Its sorrel-like leaves are pretty and no nuisance and the bulbs do well and increase in any dryish, sunny place.

Schizostylis. With its spikes of miniature gladioli-like flowers, this is a useful autumn-blooming plant that is hardy as far north as St Andrews. In colder districts it should be grown in a sunny border near the house. Elsewhere it is happy in the average border so long as the soil is reasonably moist. *S. coccinea* and its form 'Gigantea' have crimson flowers; there is an excellent pink form, 'Mrs Hegarty', and a paler, late-flowering form 'Viscountess Byng' which blooms from Noevmber to severe frost. This latter is too late for all but mild districts.

Scilla. The charming little bright-blue scillas of spring are known and loved by everybody. (See also *Endymion hispanicus*, formerly *Scilla campanulata*.)

Tulipa. The early-blooming species tulips last the longest in flower. Of these the best are the hybrids of *kaufmanniana* the water lily tulip, the *praestans* hybrids, and those of *greigii*. Individual varieties on offer change from year to year but it is best to choose the shorter, less top-

D

heavy types. My advice is to avoid the *fosterianas*, with their large blooms that soon shatter, and to select the shorter *praestans* multi-flowered reds, any kaufmannianas you can get and the less expensive of the greigiis which have particularly beautifully marked foliage and very shapely blooms.

With regard to the taller, more conventional tulips, in order to en-sure not missing them entirely if one is away when they flower, it is wisest to plant a succession of the different types. The early doubles, though not graceful, are long-lasting. Some early singles such as the orange 'De Wet' will grow in grass and continue for many years. The cottage tulips are sturdier and seem to last longer than the later Darwins but the lily-flowered varieties of the Darwins are too good to miss. Late planting helps to avoid Tulip Fire disease and the ideal practice is to dig them up and dry them off when the foliage has withered, and replant the bulbs each year in a different site.

SIX

Self-gardening Beds and Borders

The counsel of perfection for the absent gardener is to plan and mulch his beds and borders so that they keep down weeds, shelter each other from the wind and virtually look after themselves. Beds so treated can be most attractive and colourful throughout the year, provided suitable plants are chosen.

Obviously, the ground must be well cleaned, and enriched with suitable compost before planting. After that, mulching to keep down the weeds will also prevent drought and add nutriment to the soil until the leaves touch and the plants maintain themselves.

Alternatively, the pebble-bed method (discussed already in Chapter Two) can be used—enriching the ground with compost, incorporating a sprinkling of charcoal to keep the earth sweet, adding well-soaked peat to retain moisture and improve the soil structure, and covering the bed or border with heavy black polythene. Crosses should then be cut for the insertion of plants and the polythene should finally be covered with an attractive layer of shale or pebbles. Beds so treated will be free of any need for maintenance for several years. When the soil starts to warm up in spring is the best time for constructing pebble-beds in the colder parts of the country. In the south and west, September and October will give satisfactory results.

Many of the plants already suggested are suitable either for pebble-beds or for self-maintaining borders. For a bed to be trouble-free without using the polythene covering, a high proportion of weed-suppressors must be used to cover the ground beneath the specimen shrubs and trees. Many such ground-covering plants have already been listed in Chapter Three. To them I would add for foreground planting the helianthemums, those tiny rock-roses which, if sheared over after flowering, keep close and compact and make a ground-hugging carpet in any well-drained place as well as carrying a long succession of prettily coloured small saucer flowers in summer. The best helianthemums for the purpose are the soft-red 'Ben Dearg', the yellow 'Ben Fhada', the orange 'Ben Mare', the soft-pink 'Rhodanthe Carneum', the nasturtium-orange 'Taylor's Seedling', and 'Wisley Primrose'. After about seven or eight years the plants may become straggly and should then be renewed, but as they are comparatively inexpensive to buy this need not cause great hardship.

PEBBLE-BEDS

Subjects with aristocratic foliage set off the pebbles best. Spiky-leaved plants like irises, the statuesque yucca, libertia, sisyrinchium and dwarf bamboo make striking contrasts with the rounded foliage of the bergenias whose leaves will usually add winter orange and pinky-scarlet when grown among pebbles and in full sun. Hostas will find in sharp-edged stones the protection from slugs their lovely leaves deserve. Plants can be selected for effect, and one should aim to build up a balanced, interesting yet unified planting. To this end the plants should be set in tiers, the tallest towards the back of the border or in the middle of an island bed—the medium growers next, and so on. Plants of spreading and attractive habit should be used in the foreground to set off the pebbles. Particularly effective in such a planting is a tree trained wisteria grown on a short leg (as a standard, that is, rather than a climber). We had in our previous garden a ten-year old plant which grew to more than 1·1 m (3½ ft) high and was attractively gnarled, forming an assymetrical umbrella-shape, rather like the trees in the Chinese landscape of a willow-pattern plate. It came as an ordinary climbing wisteria from the nursery, then for the first few years we stopped all the side shoots at three buds from the main stem, allowing two leaders to twine around the stake. Year by year we pinch back secondary shoots to the second bud. In three years the little tree had started to flower; in five it had assumed its characteristic habit and was beautiful with its pleasing foliage and swinging chains of bloom. Either the lavender-blue *Wisteria sinensis* or the bronze-leaved *W. venusta*, with chubby white racemes are suitable.

On acid soils the dwarf rhododendrons and such associates as the Japanese maples, ericas, callunas, daboecias and mahonias make fine subjects for either self-maintaining, or polythene-covered beds. They should be given a spongy, acid-reacting compost containing peat, leaf-mould from an acid site or rotted bracken.

Dwarf rhododendrons for beds and borders form into two main groups: the species and the hybrids. Of the species, the members of the *Rhododendron lapponicum* series provide a delightful range of plants for sunny and open places. If grown in shade or under the drip of trees they become leggy and lichenous. Perhaps the best known of the lapponicums are the blues such as *R. impeditum* which forms a compact mound of steely-emerald foliage and lavender-blue flowers, The starry little blooms of *R. intricatum* are of similar colouring, and there is the deeper almost royal blue of *scintillans* and the lavender hue of *hippophaeoides*. These form bushes of from 30 to 60 cm (1 to 2 ft) high and wide. Good associates for them are the bronze-leafed yellow *R. chryseum*, and the white *R. microleucum* which, with the red-violet *R. lysolepis* make an attractive colour combination. These bloom in early May.

Flowering a little earlier, *Rhododendron racemosum* is a pretty pink. Different forms of this species vary in height but 'Forrest 19404' is a reliable dwarf with paler-centred, deep-pink-edged tiny butterfly blooms. Should any form become too tall it may be pruned back, as it will shoot again from lower down the stem, and so may be easily kept within the context of the group.

Quite different is the quaint *R. campylogynum* with little thimble flowers on arching stalks. This is rather later to flower and is useful to continue the season of interest. In height, and in the winter red-purple of its foliage colour, it firs in well with a group of lapponicums. A good *R. campylogynum* is plum-purple in colour but forms may be obtained with salmon-pink or crushed-strawberry flowers. Both of these are pleasing but there are also yellows which are usually poor and muddy in colour.

To extend the season into June and even July the *R. saluenense* series is useful. First to bloom of these is the rosy-purple *R. calostrotum* with the typical open salver-shaped flowers of the group. It is usually in bloom in May with *R. campylogynum*. The similar but brighter *R. keleticum* follows in June with *R. nitens* still later in July. There is a particularly good form in a dusky pinky-rose shade which is sometimes available. A useful little creeping member of the series is *R. radicans* which flowers in late May or June. Unlike the others this needs a moist and rather shady spot—the bottom of a north slope or the north side of a large boulder suits it well.

Also liking half shade is *R. hanceanum* 'Nanum', one of the choicest of dwarf yellows with dark shiny pointed leaves and quite large primrose-coloured, orange-anthered flowers. It needs a rather more sheltered situation than the others mentioned. *R. sargentianum*, too, is yellow in colour and is easy to grow in the north and west but difficult in hotter, drier gardens in the south.

Generally larger in form, leaf and flower than the species are the hybrids of three main groups—the blue *lapponicum* hybrids, the round-leafed *williamsianum* crosses and the reds, most of which have *forrestii repens* as one parent.

Of the dwarf blue hybrids, the best known and least satisfactory is 'Blue Tit' which needs sun to flower freely. The smallest, neatest and best of the blues is probably Sapphire which makes a 60 cm (2 ft) mound in most gardens. 'Blue Diamond' is deeper in colour and excellent in every way, but it can grow tall. It stands clipping occasionally, even though this may result in loss of bloom for a year, and can well be kept at a height of 90 cm (3 ft). It is one that I would not like to be without. Also tall but not reaching more than 1·5 m (5 ft) in height, 'Augfast' is a good dark, lavender blue. Neither of these last two have more than a 1·5 m (5 ft) spread, and take many years to attain their full size. All have small, neat leaves and a pleasant mounded habit.

The *williamsianum* hybrids as a whole need more wind-shelter than the blues. They have a mounded, neat habit of up to 1·2 m (4 ft), and rounded, pretty leaves. Among the best are 'Humming Bird', in cherry crimson with dark green leaves; 'Moonstone', in creamy, pink-tinged yellow; the excellent yellow 'Cowslip'; and the striking Persian-rose 'Temple Belle'. This looks particularly well with 'Blue Diamond' for contrast.

Of the red hybrids of *repens*, 'Elizabeth' is undoubtedly the best small garden rhododendron of all time, with bright red trumpets and neat, dark green leaves. It is, though, much bigger than any of those mentioned so far and with its ultimate height of 1·5 m (5 ft) and a spread of nearly 2 m (6 ft), it is more of a background rhododendron. For a smaller planting its 30 cm (12 in) high clone 'Jenny' is more suitable—at its best tumbling down a shady slope. The other dwarf red hybrids are sometimes shy of flowering as are some forms of *repens* itself.

Another attractive plant is 'Yellow Hammer'—a slender, more upright grower with very small leaves and, in the best form, small bronzy-yellow bells that contrast and cool the scarlet of 'Elizabeth' in an admirable way.

Where a larger plant is wanted 'Fabia' in its various forms can be relied upon to arouse interest in striking shades of terracotta. My own favourite is 'Roman Pottery' which is a softened version of the colour that its name implies, but 'Tangerine' and 'Tower Court' are also good.

Of the larger growers, for the sake of their pretty, blue-tinted leaves and delightful hanging bell-like flowers I would certainly include one of the 'Lady Chamberlain' or 'Lady Rosebery' clones. To extend the season into July, 'Romany Chai' or 'Vesuvius' would bring in a colour note near to geranium-scarlet in tone. Where early frosts are a risk worth taking, the butterfly lilac flowers of 'Praecox' will always please and this hybrid should be succeeded where space allows by the similar 'Emasculum' which blooms a fortnight later. In milder gardens the old *caucasicum* hybrid 'Nobleanum' should be planted so that its crimson globes may open in frost-free periods from Christmas on.

For very exposed or frosty gardens some of the above may be a bad risk but such are luckily in the minority and for them an answer may be found in the wide range of iron-hard rhododendrons now beginning to trickle into this country from Germany where Herr Deitrich Hobbie has been breeding them at Linswege, which lies between the Weser and the Ems and is open to the cold Scandinavian winds and to much lower temperatures than are to be experienced in Britain. Herr Hobbie has used the proved 'best parent' species *wardii*, *forrestii* var. *repens*, *haematodes*, *dichroanthum*, *williamsianum* and others to cross with old 'hardy hybrids' such as 'Britannia', 'Cunningham's Sulphur', 'Doncaster' to raise a race of extra-tough ironclads with the dwarf habit, neat leaves and pure colouring of their species parents. The first of these crosses are now available in Britain. 'Elizabeth Hobbie', one of Herr Hobbie's *forrestii* var. *repens* crosses, has proved itself reliable in our own garden and though for brilliance of colour and elegance of truss I would still choose 'Elizabeth', the German 'Elizabeth Hobbie' with its dense, compact habit, deep red flowers without a trace of blue and neat, dark, weatherproof leaves is a better choice for the bleak frost-ridden garden than many of the older 'hardy hybrids' with their giant growth and dull-looking leaves which often become tatty with the rigours to which they are exposed.

For more average garden climates, a different line of development offers an exciting promise in the new hybrids resulting from the crossing of the hardier members of the *Triflorum* series with some of the charming members of the *Cinnabarinum* series. The resultant crosses, so far, have small graceful, blue-green leaves rendering them easy to grow in most gardens as they are not as susceptible to the effects of drought and wind as larger-leaved rhododendrons. With the mountain-dwelling species of the *Triflorum* series as parent (which often grow to a height of nearly 4,000 m (12,000 ft) in extremely rigorous conditions in their natural habitat in Tibet and in Yunnan) they are naturally able to withstand reasonable exposure in British gardens. Two of the best, so far, are the luscious, rhodamine-purple to deep-lilac 'Yunncinn' and the delightful pinky-apricot 'Alison Johnstone'. Both have neat trusses of the *Triflorum* series with the related azalea-like flower shape—widely open and showing an attractive flare of stamens. Both have also the appealing blueish leaf-sheen of the *Cinnabarinum* parent.

South-facing pebble beds will naturally be used to offer sun-lovers a home. Here one can show off the handsome *Fatsia japonica*, the castor oil plant, with its sculptured palmate leaves, or the 'Variegata' form with creamy margined foliage. The stately yucca, too, will be happy complemented by the spiky-leaved *Iris pallida* 'Variegata', the pretty hebes, rosemary, perovskia, sage and golden marjoram. In such a position *Lavandula stoechas*, the chunky-headed lavender from the Mediterranean maquis, should thrive.

Other good plants would be the grey-leafed *Phlomis fruticosa*; the smaller-growing evergreen conifers; *Chaenomeles × superba*, or the dwarf *C. japonica* with its attractively sprawling habit and terracotta scarlet flowers in early spring; the uncommon *Erinacea anthyllis* (*pungens*) hedgehog broom, with its hummock of spiny branches and misty-blue pea flowers; and the prostrate broom, *Cytisus × kewensis*, with its water-fall of primrose flowers.

The modern fashion for placing herbaceous plants in an island bed in the lawn has never appealed to me because of the bare and stubbly appearance many such plantings have in the winter months. However, at Ness Gardens in the Wirral, there are island beds with a new look. At the University of Liverpool Botanic Gardens, lightly built shrubs are used to form the backbone of such beds, surrounded by an outward froth of herbaceous plantings.

Island pebble-beds should be sited in the open to encourage sturdy and symmetrical growth. As the shrubs grow, part of the outer plant-ing of each bed will be in the shade and there such characterful shade-lovers as the hostas, heucheras, tiarellas, hardy cyclamen, *Alchemilla mollis*, candelabra primulas, and hellebores can be accommodated.

The choice of shrubs to form the hard core of the beds requires careful thought. Some evergreens or evergreys should be used so that the beds are not too bare in the winter, while towards the edges on the sunnier side evergreen perennials such as bergenias may be placed together with such sun-loving dwarf sub-shrubs as helianthemums and heathers to balance the lasting leaves of the hellebores and cyclamen in the shaded aspect. As backbone shrubs the hardier cistus such as *C. × cyprius*, with its spectacularly blotched white petals, and *C. laurifolius* are ideal, as also are *Senecio greyi* of the grey leaves and lemon-yellow 'daisies', *Phlomis fruticosa*, *Elaeagnus × ebbingei* and *E. pungens* 'Variegata' to give year-round foliage interest. With them might be used such lighter-built deciduous shrubs as the dwarf *Philadelphus microphyllus*—mock orange, the hardy *Fuchsia* 'Riccartonii', potentillas, and *Hypericum* 'Hidcote'.

Supporting herbaceous plantings should be of subjects that do not need staking, though with the availability now of circular wire supports through which the plants grow and which they completely hide with their foliage by the middle of June, there is no reason why a group or two of any specially desired subjects should not be included. Most of the species geraniums are self-supporting and among the best are the pink *G. endressii* growing to about a foot, the double blue *G. pratense* 'Cacrulea Plena', and the more compact 'Johnson's Blue'. Sedums such as *S. spectabile* 'Autumn Joy' and the purple foliaged *S. maximum* 'Atropurpureum' are good value, as are the day lilies.

Bergenias are valuable, from glamorous 'Ballawley' ('Delbees') with 30 cm (1ft) wide leaves to the glossy green paddles of the humbler × *smithii*. The leaves of *B. purpurascens* turn to rosy beetroot in winter making a wonderful foil to the verdigris-blue foliage of one of the junipers. The German bergenia cultivars are good and 'Abendglut' has foliage that turns to bronzy-red in cold weather while its rose-crimson flower spikes are often borne in autumn as well as spring. The neat-growing, warm-pink 'Morgenröte' also flowers twice a year. *Salvia superba*, and the handsome-foliaged *Ligularia* 'Desdemona' with its plum-lined leaves and bright orange, solidly textured heads of 'daisy' flowers, will both give long-lasting notes of interest. *Miscanthus sinensis* 'Zebrinus', the zebra grass, is handsome with its bands of yellow across its tall leaves. Like the 'dwarf' 1·2 to 1·5 m (4 to 5 ft) form, 'Pumila', of *Cortaderia selloana*, the pampas grass, it can be very effective in an island pebble-bed.

Sited away from trees, and with curved outlines that perhaps pick up and echo the flowing lines of a nearby border, an island pebble-bed can greatly enhance the charm and interest of even the smallest garden. In larger plots the use of two or three can give a largish lawn the feel and charm of a garden glade.

For use either with or without a polythene-and-pebble covering, other tall and statuesque plants such as *Cynara scolymus*, the globe artichoke; *Mahonia japonica* and *M.* 'Charity'; *Osmunda regalis*, the royal fern, and acanthus are all very effective.

PLANTING ACCORDING TO SOIL AND ASPECT

If one decides to dispense with the polythene idea and still plant with an eye to self-maintenance, it is important to base each bed or border on the 'commune' principle, choosing subjects which are by nature suited to the particular soil, site and aspect. As explained in Chapter Four, much of a weekend gardener's success consists in suiting the plants to the site, growing quantities of what will do well and thrive without attention in that particular situation. The following suggestions will supplement advice given in that earlier chapter.

In full sun, the cistuses, phlomis, hebes, rosemary, lavender, sages, rugosa roses, perovskia, *Viburnum farreri* (*fragrans*), ceanothus, cytisus, *Erinacea anthyllis* (*pungens*), *Genista lydia*, *Hypericum* 'Hidcote', *H. olympicum*, and—near the sea—the shrubby *H. balearicum*, with libertia, bergenia and scrambling clematis would associate well with heliantheums, thymes, golden marjoram and teucrium to form a trouble-free community.

In shade, ferns, hostas, candelabra primulas, day lilies, hellebores, rodgersias (if the soil is moist), *Mahonia* 'Undulata' and *M. japonica*, chaenomeles, *Garrya elliptica*, laurustinus and camellias (on acid soil) would help each other to keep down weeds.

On acid soils, rhododendrons and azaleas, gaultheria, Japanese maples, berberis, heaths, ling, vaccinium, lace-cap hydrangea, skimmia, rugosa roses and birch would form self-maintaining colonies.

For alkaline sites, viburnums, cherries, crabs, musk roses, rugosas, clematis, hellebore, *Daphne mezereum*, cotoneaster, philadelphus, weigela, hardy geranium, nepeta, alchemilla, day lily and kniphofia would combine with cistus and rosemary to do their own 'gardening' in a similar way.

The more vigorous-growing dwarf alpines may be massed in self-gardening beds and borders, and are attractive to edge a terrace or line a path or drive, giving the weekend garden a cared-for well-maintained look, although in fact being almost entirely self-supporting. They will thrive on the level in well-drained soil or may be planted to cover a rocky slope. Among those which are self-sufficient enough to keep down weeds are:

Aethionema 'Warley Rose'; *Ajuga reptans* 'Variegata'; *Alyssum saxatile* (in variety); *Arabis albida* 'Plena' (double white); *Armeria maritima*; aubrieta; *Campanula garganica* 'W. H. Paine' (white) and 'Fenestrella' (pale blue); dianthus such as 'Bombardier' (scarlet), 'Elizabeth' (pink) and 'Grace Mather' (salmon); *Gentiana septemoda* and *G. lagodechiana*; helianthemum; *Hypericum olympicum*; hyssop; Lithospermum 'Heavenly Blue' (on acid soils only); *Phlox subulata* 'Betty' (pale pink), 'G. F. Wilson' (lavender). and 'Sampson' (deep pink); *Polygonum vacciniifolium*; prunella; mossy saxifrages such as 'Flowers of Sulphur', 'Sir Douglas Haig' (crimson), and 'Knappington Pink'; *Sedum spurium* 'Coccineum' (red); *Teucrium chamaedrys* (pale pink), *T. lithospermifolium* (crimson);

Veronica rupestris and *Zauschneria californica*, the Californian fuchsia (in a dry, sunny spot). Among these may be planted any small spring bulbs one fancies, including the dwarf daffodils. Plant through the mats of foliage, taking out sufficient soil with an apple corer to make the holes in which to insert the bulbs.

Edgings and borders of heaths may be almost equally effective, although on alkaline soils these must be restricted to *Erica carnea* and its varieties and *E.* × *darleyensis*, with the possible additions of *E. ciliaris* and *E. vagans* 'Mrs D. F. Maxwell' on soils which are not too hot and shallow.

SEVEN

Seaside Gardens

Many weekend gardeners have their retreats at the seaside. For some twelve years, my husband and I lived within a quarter of a mile of the North Wales coast overlooking the Isle of Anglesey, and open to the south-westerly gales. Before that we gardened for a time in Cornwall, close to the Carrick Roads, and equally subject to salt-laden gales in summer and winter, and cold easterly winds in spring.

Wind, salt and blown sand are the main hazards that the seaside gardener has to face. Against them one must plant for outer wind-breaks and shelter, subjects that grow in nature near to the sea and have adapted themselves over thousands of years to resist its attack. With such shelter to filter the worst of the salt-laden gales, spray and the rasping blast of blown sand, one can plant other, less tough desirables. The climate of the western coastline of Britain varies a great deal from that of the east coast, but these factors are common to both. Apart from that, along the western coastline one can often succeed in growing choice and tender plants. On the east, subject to the icy sweeps of winds from the Continental land mass during the winter, only the hardies can be attempted.

Many of our best wind- and salt-resisters come from New Zealand, where they have to suffer the onslaught of salty spray and sand borne by the gales that sweep from the Pacific Ocean and the Tasman Sea. Many such coastal plants have grey, hairy leaves—the function of the tiny hairs being to prevent the salt crystals from reaching the leaf sur-face. The rain quickly causes the salt, trapped in the hairs, to fall to the ground. Some New Zealand shrubs have hairs only on the under surface while the upper surface has a high gloss, the glossy film pre-venting the leaves from absorbing the salt or becoming caked with sand. Euonymus and pittosporum are typical examples. Other New Zealanders such as the hebes have a particularly tough, doubled skin.

Escallonia macrantha which grows on the coast in Chile exudes a sticky gum to protect the leaf surface. Only those escallonias that possess this sticky resinous quality will succeed right on the coast in the full lash of the storms. The others—including most of the hybrids—must be grown within the outer shelter.

Gardens at beach level suffer not only from the wind and spray but also from the invasion of sand from the shore and dunes. Salt-laden sand will often blow a mile or more inland, but it is not only the salt which is harmful; there is the blast of the sand which chisels at the stems and leaves. Thick ground cover is the gardener's best ally in beachside gardens, using plants which will grow in almost pure sand and are dense enough to trap the sand and prevent the wind picking it up to bury other plantings. Burnet roses, rugosa roses, *Mesembryanthemum edule* (in the south and west) and *Hypericum calycinum* (for the north and east) are excellent for this purpose. Even the invasive *Campanula poscharkyana* well earns its place.

Often the weekend gardener may not be at home to hose down his plants after a salt-laden gale so he must choose outer defences that the storm cannot damage, which will protect his treasures in his absence. In the following list † denotes tenderness, while * is used to denote those shrubs which will act as shelter and withstand the full force of wind and spray.

Shrubs for sand include †*Abelia* × *grandiflora*; †*Abutilon vitifolium*; †*Acacia rhetinodes*, autumn-flowering mimosa; *Arundinaria japonica* (a bamboo which may spread too enthusiastically on wet, acid soils but which makes a useful and impenetrable 2 to 3 m (7 to 10 ft) protective screen on sand); berberis; buddleia (not for driest areas); caryopteris; cassinia, golden shrubby heath; chaenomeles; choisya; cistus (not fully hardy but can cope even with salt spray; they should be set close in groups to protect each other against frost and spray); colutea, bladder senna; †*Coronilla glauca*; *Cortaderia cordata*, pampas grass; *Cotinus coggygria*; cotoneaster; *elaeagnus*; *Erinacea anthyllis* (*pungens*); *Escallonia macrantha*; *Euonymus japonicus*; *Fabiana violacea* and *F. imbricata* 'Prostrata'; *Fatsia japonica*; fuchsia (hardy sorts); garrya; *griselinia; *hebe; *Hippophae rhamnoides*, sea buckthorn; hydrangea (on limy sand the hydrangea may need treating with Murphy Sequesterene), *Hypericum calycinum; *hyssop; *juniper; lavender; *lavatera; †leptospermum; *Lonicera japonica halliana* (about the only situation in which the planting of this invasive honeysuckle is warranted is to clothe a fence or screen to keep out wind and salt); *Lupinus arboreus*, tree lupin; *Mahonia aquifolium*; †*Olearia albida* (toughest of the scented daisy bushes) and †*O. macrodonta* (which is much more pleasing with its steely holly-like leaves that are silvery underneath, but it will not stand full exposure);

osmarea; perovskia; philadelphus; phlomis (not hardy enough for the most bitter north-eastern exposures but will thrive elsewhere if clipped back after flowering in June); *Phormium tenax*, New Zealand flax with crowns of huge, sword-like leaves and arching spikes of dull, coppery-red flowers; †pittosporum (*P. ralphii* is tough enough to use for shelter in the south, or the west in milder locales; it was not hardy with us near Llandudno, but will grow in the Lleyn Peninsula and the west of Scotland); potentilla; pyracantha; romneya, California poppy, with beautiful but fleeting blooms over a long period; rosemary; ruta, rue; salvia; *santolina; *senecio; solanum; *Spiraea × vanhouttei*; symphori-carpus; *tamarix; teucrium; thyme; *Viburnum tinus*, *V. × burkwoodii* and *V. carlesii* and *Yucca filamentosa*.

Often in very windy gardens, or to protect choice plantings such as rhododendrons (as in the west of Scotland), artificial screening is used to help the shelter become established. Coir-netting, wattles and lath fencing make good artificial wind-breaks of this type. Another idea, which gives more permanent protection, is to build an earth-filled wall and top it with hardy, fairly compact shrubs such as gorse and hebes. Even in the smallest garden dwarf shrubs of the hebe family may be used to give temporary shelter to new plantings, later being moved to shelter other additions or to a more permanent position.

In large gardens and where there is room, an outer belt of salt-resisting trees may be planted to give additional shelter. Suitable for this purpose are common sycamore; hawthorn, *Cupressus macrocarpa* 'Lutea' (the golden variety of this species is more wind-tolerant than the green); ash; the tender *Olearia traversii* (Cornwall and Western Isles only); *Picea sitchensis*, the Sitka spruce; *Pinus contorta*, *P. nigra austriaca* (supremely hardy even for the north-east), the dwarf *P. mugo* (which will grow even with its feet in salt water), *P. pinaster*, the Bournemouth pine (only suitable for the west and south) and *P. radiata* (mild areas); *Populus alba*; *Quercus ilex*, the holm oak; *Salix alba* and *S. caprea*, and *Sorbus aria*.

Within these may be planted a shelter belt of shrubs such as the bamboo, *Arundinaria japonica* (which is an excellent wind-filter and may readily be extended by detaching individual root shoots and laying them full length in trenches 15 cm (6 in) deep in May when shoots will quickly arise from each joint); *Atriplex halimus*, 1·5 m (5 ft) with pretty grey, wind-rippled leaves; *Aucuba japonica*; *Cistus × pulverulentus* (*crispus*) (for mild areas) and *C. laurifolius* (hardy in most maritime exposures); *Elaeagnus × ebbingei*; *Escallonia* 'Exoniensis' (white-flowered, mild areas, 4 m (12 ft)), *E.* 'Crimson Spire' which reaches 2 m (6 ft) and *E. macrantha* (the best for full exposure, 4 m (12 ft)); *Euonymus japonicus*; griselinia; *Hebe brachysiphon*, 1·2 m (4 ft), *H. dieffenbachii*, 90 cm (3 ft) and *H. franciscana* 'Blue Gem', 90 cm (3 ft); *Hippophae rhamnoides*; *Phormium tenax*; *Sambucus nigra*, elder; *Senicio greyi* 1·2 m (4 ft); *Tamarix gallica*; *Ulex europaeus*, gorse, 1·5 m (5 ft), and *Ulex europaeus* 'Plenus', 1·2 m (4 ft) with double flowers.

Where the heights have not been given the shrubs will grow to about 2 m (6 ft) and upwards but can be topped as required.

Hedges may be grown from the vigorous *Cupressocyparis leylandii* but this, like its parent *Cupressus macrocarpa*, suffers from browning in full exposure and should only be used where there is protection from full off-sea gales. Plants should be set 75 cm (2½ ft) apart and cannot be satisfactorily topped at less than 2·5 m (8 ft). Hybrid broom seedlings make an effective hedge if set out at 45 cm (18 in). After flowering they should be levelled with the shears and the sides trimmed to remove as many seed pods as possible. The second year they should be again cut back—to about 45 cm (18 in)—and again trimmed. After that they can be allowed to achieve the desired height. Sod and stone 'hedges'—the bank-type boundaries of Cornwall and the Isle of Man—are useful to give additional height and shelter, and they can be decorative if topped with hebes, gorse or broom, their sides being planted with primroses and other wild flowers.

Perennial plants for seaside planting, all with a long season of flower or interest, include:
Achillea 'Moonshine' and 'Coronation Gold'; *Alstroemeria aurantiaca*, the common form of the Peruvian lily; *Anaphalis*; the ground covering *Anthemis cupaniana* with its pretty silver filigree foliage, *A. tinctoria* 'Mrs E. C. Buxton' and *A. sancti-johannis*; areneria (for ground cover); *Armeria maritima*, thrift; *Artemisia abrotanum*, southernwood, *A. canescens* (prostrate), and *A. absinthium* 'Lambrook Silver'; *Asphodeline lutea*; aubrieta; bergenia; *Borago laxiflora* (ground cover with pretty pale blue flowers, like a tiny Chinaman's hat, in June-July); campanula; centranthus; valerian; chrysanthemum; *Convolvulus mauritanicus* (a lovely trailer for mild areas in full sun with lavender-blue flowers) and *C. cneorum* (with silver foliage and white flowers); *Cynara*, globe artichoke and giant thistle; dianthus; dictamnus; dimorphotheca (osteospermum), the pretty mat-forming African daisy with large, glistening-petalled flowers, white with a blue central zone in *D. ecklonensis* and pink in *D. barberiae*; echinops; erigeron (especially the dwarfer forms which make low mats of growth covered with substantial numbers of 'daisies'; eryngium; sea holly; geranium (hardy, also the bedding perlargoniums, particularly the pretty ivy-leafed forms which will often survive the

winter against a wall in mild areas); gypsophila; hemerocallis, day lily; iberis; kniphofia; lathyrus (the everlasting pea makes an attractive climber or scrambler); limonium, sea lavender; linum; lupin; *Macleaya cordata*, the tall imposing plume poppy; malva, mallow; nepeta, oenothera, the evening primrose; oriental poppy; *Phygelius capensis*, cape figwort; *Polygonum affine* (ground cover); salvia; sedum; *Stachys lanata*; *Stokesia laevis* 'Blue Star'; *Teucrium chamaedrys* (low hummocks); thyme; verbascum (woolly-leafed spires); wallflower and *Zauschneria californica*.

In mild areas, many unusual and exciting shrubs and climbers can be grown, including varieties of the eucalyptus; *Acacia dalrympleana*, mimosa; tender jasmines; plumbago; the brilliant-flowered campsis; metrosideros, Australasian bottle-brush; cassia and many others. Readers are recommended to borrow T. Arnold-Forster's *Trees and Shrubs for the Milder Countries* from their regional library or via the RHS library.

Drought, water restrictions and above-average sunshine have not made the gardener's lot any easier during the last few years, and particularly is this true of seaside gardens where strong winds and sandy soil tend to exacerbate the problem.

Soil in seaside gardens tends to be poor as well as sandy, so it is important to improve the texture. As with other problem areas, digging in all available moisture-holding humus can help a great deal. Seaweed, which is free and an excellent source of humus, may be added to the soil along with garden compost, farmyard manure, spent hops, mushroom compost or moss peat.

Cut dried bracken (see also p. 25) should be used as a protective mulch spread over the vegetable garden, around shrubs and on flower beds during the winter to protect the soil from salt and blown sand. Applied over a layer of fallen leaves, it is wonderfully nutritious, and as it rots it improves the soil structure.

EIGHT

Vegetables for the Weekend Gardener

Anyone with an out-of-town garden will find it worth while to grow some vegetables and fruit. Today, more than ever, it makes economic sense to be as self-supporting as possible, quite apart from the enjoyment and benefit to be derived from eating garden produce so fresh that the vitamins have not had time to leach away.

For too many garden-owners, the be-all and end-all of the country vegetable plot seems to be the growing of peas. Far too many rows are sown and the result is often an indigestible glut. Every cook knows that the best-flavoured vegetables are those picked before the gardener thinks that they are ready. Unless you can be sure of getting down to your garden every weekend, there will not be much point in growing quick-developing vegetables such as lettuces, peas or broad beans, which must be picked at their peak. A couple of weeks' absence, and you may well return to find bolting lettuces and hard-as-bullets peas and beans. The same applies to strawberries, and those who spend the main part of their lives in town might more profitably set up a strawberry barrel or tower-pot system that would take up little space on the flat balcony or the town-house patio and yield ready-to-hand fruit during the week. Tomato plants, too, could be set in Gro-Bags to take up little space and give fresh tomatoes for weekday salads. The clever weekender will work out the best use of his backyard patio, window box or balcony, along with that of his out-of-town garden so that one supplements the other. Mint, thyme, sage, parsley and chives, for instance, may be common to both, so that there are always herbs available to suit the culinary needs. Weekenders who want to make the most of their opportunities to grow part of their diet in town, might find helpful my *Window Box and Container Gardening* and *Backyards and Tiny Gardens*, both published by Fabers and the latter in paperback.

By far the best returns for the weekender come from long-season crops such as potatoes, brassica, root vegetables, and from long-lasting fruit such as apples, keeping varieties of pear and rhubarb. To these one might add the gooseberry because if you know you are going to be away from your garden for two or three weeks just when the fruit is about to ripen, you can pick the gooseberries green and let them ripen slowly in the window of your town house or flat.

With all vegetables, the absent gardener's main problem will be that of drought. To offset this it is essential to line planting trenches and holes either with well-soaked peat or with layers of folded and soaked newspaper. Straw mulches applied when the ground is wet will help to retain moisture and the straw can later be composted with excellent results.

STAR CROPS FOR WEEKEND GARDENS

Spinach. This is a popular vegetable with the dietary-enlightened but weekend gardeners might find spinach beet or the drought-resistant New Zealand spinach more satisfactory for their purpose. The leaves of either, if picked fresh and put into an airtight polythene bag, will keep throughout the week in the refrigerator.

Both spinach beet and New Zealand spinach need well-manured ground. The spinach beet will tolerate some shade but must be kept away from marrows or cucumbers which might infect it with virus diseases.

Spinach beet. This should be sown in March-April and will crop through the summer and autumn, often continuing through the winter until late May. During the winter it should be protected with bracken if possible in order to improve the quality of the leaves. It is otherwise quite hardy.

New Zealand spinach. Exceptionally drought-resistant, this is the best choice for sandy or chalky, sharply drained gardens, or sites that tend to dry out. Less hardy than the spinach beet, it should be sown outdoors in mid-May. For an earlier crop you could raise a few pots of seedlings on a town windowsill, gradually harden them off on the balcony or in the yard and plant them out in the weekend garden in the middle of May. Unlike spinach beet, New Zealand spinach will not withstand the winter, so any surplus should be stripped before the autumn frosts are expected and either cooked and eaten, or put in the freezer. In mild areas it will often be found to have seeded itself, reappearing the following year.

Shallots. These are more easy to manage than onions. They have a shorter growing season and, being smaller and better keeping, can more easily be taken up to town for later use. The only disadvantage is that they do not succeed in heavy clays, so heavy soils should be lightened by the addition of ashes, peat, and so on.

Fresh manure should never be used when preparing the ground for shallots. Deeply worked, well-drained, sandy, gravelly, chalky, or light loamy soils are best. The bulbs may be planted in January in mild areas, but should wait until February or even March elsewhere; 500 g (1 lb) of shallots is sufficient for a 4·5 m (15 ft) row. (Each bulb multiplies into nine or ten shallots.) Some strains are infected with virus so avoid cheap offers, buying the bulbs only from a reputable source.

The shallots should be lifted when the foliage starts to yellow in July, and should be dried out of doors for a few days before being stored in an airy place in trays or in nets. They will keep until the following May or June. Some may also be kept to provide sets for the following year.

Potatoes. In small gardens only the earliest types are really worth growing. 'Ulster Chieftain' is an excellent variety, but not one for keeping. However, if you have a large garden or land you want to clean before bringing it into general cultivation and can borrow or hire a mechanical cultivator, the later sorts may also be grown. Potatoes need an open site, free from frost. A deep, well-drained, medium loam is ideal, but they will grow on most soils and tolerate acid conditions well.

The potato plot, ideally, should have been manured the previous autumn, but where this has been omitted, compost or seaweed dug in before planting will help.

Certified seed potatoes should be bought in February and set up in seed trays, 'rose' end upwards to chit. The young sprouts should be strong and greeny purple, and about 2·5 cm (1 in) long before planting. They should be set out in March or early April according to district. The earliest plantings give the highest yields.

It is worth while, also, to plant some of the tubers in barrels, or stone troughs or sinks. The tubers should be set about 5 cm (2 in) below the soil surface, packing straw around the outside of the container and encasing the whole in black polythene to force early growth. Once the shoots are well through and the danger of frost is past, the covering can gradually be folded back and then removed. Care must be taken to inspect the barrels when visiting the garden and to water them if necessary. Whether grown in the open or in barrels, once the potato plants are 10 to 15 cm (4 to 6 in) high, soil should be mounded over the foliage until only the tops are exposed. This not only supports the plants but prevents the potatoes 'greening', checks weeds, and encourages tuber formation and growth.

Globe artichokes. The beauty of this plant is that it can be grown as an ornamental in the flower border where it will be not only highly decorative but effective at keeping down weeds.

The globe artichoke needs a sunny well-drained site and well-enriched soil. The plants should be bought in April and may be set in a group, 60 cm (2 ft) apart each way. They benefit from a spring mulch (applied when the soil is wet) to retain moisture, and should be given a liquid feed whenever the garden is visited during the summer. From July to September the heads are ready for use and should be picked before the scales start to open. Winter protection is helpful in all but the mildest areas, and can be given supplied in the form of bracken. The plants should be replaced after three seasons by offsets taken in March.

Good King Henry (poor man's asparagus). This easy, useful and flavoursome vegetable is a perennial and will grow almost anywhere, even in poor, dry soil, although it will do even better if the ground is enriched and given some moist peat to help retain moisture. Seed may be obtained from Messrs Thompson and Morgan of London Road, Ipswich, and be sown outdoors in April or May, the seedlings being thinned to 40 cm (15 in) apart. To prevent the seed rows drying out, sow in a shady but not root-ridden place, lining the seed drills with well-soaked peat. The leaves can be eaten like spinach in summer. It is the flower buds which are like asparagus and these are produced in early spring. To ensure a good crop it pays to cut the foliage back in autumn and to cover the plants with straw. Propagation is by the division of old plants.

Brassicas. This is one of the most important and rewarding families for the weekend gardener because the plants can be left at maturity for several weeks without deterioration. They are, however, all subject to the disease known as club root and must be grown in rotation with root vegetables, beans and potatoes, or green-manure crops. Brassica should occupy the same ground only one year in three (with the exception of the perennial broccoli, which may stay for three seasons in ground which has no history of club root).

To offset club root disease, land intended for the cultivation of brassica should be well enriched with compost, fish manure at 85 g (3 oz) to the square metre (about 1 sq yd), farm yard manure or seaweed, and surface-limed at 85 g (3 oz) to the square metre (about 1 sq yd).

NINE-STAR PERENNIAL BROCCOLI. This should be grown on land enriched as described above and fed with a fish fertilizer with potash content at 113 g (4 oz) to the square metre (about 1 sq yd) each April, for the years it is in production. If you cannot buy plants, try raising the seeds in a pot or box in town in April. Transfer the seedlings, setting them about 15 cm (6 in) apart into a nursery bed that has had plenty of thoroughly soaked peat forked in and is in a shady spot. Early in September the plants can go into their permanent positions at 75 cm (2½ ft) apart each way. The first small cauliflowers appear the following April or May and the plants will go on producing heads for the next three years, after which they must be pulled up and burned in May or June. The land should then be used for roots or peas and beans.

PURPLE SPROUTING BROCCOLI. This is a delicious vegetable to fill the mid-February-to-May vegetable gap. The plants should be sown in early April to May and firmly planted out in June or July at 60 cm (2 ft) apart. In exposed areas they should be earthed up as they grow in order to prevent wind rock.

If the shoots are picked when about 4 cm (1½ in) long, leaving more shoots to come to their peak later instead of stripping the plants, they will continue bearing over two months.

BRUSSELS SPROUTS. Like the sprouting broccoli, Brussels sprouts need a firm bed and should be earthed up against wind. Plants can usually be bought and they should be out in May or June on land manured the previous autumn or in early spring. Alternatively, where peas and beans are grown they can follow these without further dressing as the legumes will have added nitrogen to the soil.

If necessary the plants can be top-dressed in mid-July with a general or high-potash fertilizer. Yellowing leaves should always be removed to prevent the budding sprouts from rotting.

CABBAGE. This vegetable can be grown in variety to produce year-round greens. It needs an open, unshaded site with rich, humus-containing soil which, preferably, has been manured for a previous crop. As with all brassica, cabbages should never follow members of the same family in the same ground.

If the ground is not in good heart, well-rotted compost should be incorporated at the rate of half-a-bucketful to the square metre (just over 1 sq yd). If the ground is reasonably good, however, leave well alone as too much nourishment will result in sappy growth. If the soil is at all acid it must be limed before planting. Spring cabbage may be helped on after the winter by a dressing of nitro-chalk at 28 to 56 g (1 to 2 oz) to the square metre (about 2 sq yd). Spring cabbage can follow early potatoes, peas or beans, and should be set out in late September or October at 45 cm (18 in) apart. The stalks should be removed immediately after cutting, otherwise they will rot in the ground. Alternatively, the stems may be cut with a fairly deep cross at a distance of about 8 cm (3 in) from the ground to induce new cabbages to sprout from the stalk. This will usually result in four or five firm cabbages sprouting for summer use.

Winter cabbage is usually sown in April or May and should be planted out in very firm ground before the end of July at about 45 cm (18 in) apart.

Self-blanching celery. This can be grown where the weekend gardener does not want the trouble of taking out trenches but will enjoy pulling a head or two of celery to eat. The advantage with this type of celery is that it can be grown on the flat, does not need as much water as other types, and takes up little room. It must, however, be used before the end of October.

Like all celery, the self-blanching type needs a rich soil, and well-rotted compost or farmyard manure should be dug in at the rate of a two-gallon (9 l) bucket every square metre (about 1 sq yd). Shortly before planting, fish manure or a high-rating potash fertilizer should be lightly forked in at the rate of 113 g (4 oz) to the square metre (about 1 sq yd). Golden Self Blanching and American Green are the types to choose and can be sown in pots or window boxes in town and then planted out in summer at 30 cm (12 in) apart in rows 45 cm (18 in) apart. American Green ripens later than the Golden Self Blanching, generally becoming ready for eating in early October, so both should be grown to provide a succession.

A mulch of straw among the plants will help to whiten the stems and also to retain moisture.

Carrots. This vegetable does best in light, stone-free soil. Seed should never be sown on freshly manured land or the roots will split. As carrots take some time to come through after sowing, it pays to mark the rows by sowing radishes among them. The radishes can be pulled and eaten before the carrots need their space. Short horn carrots can be sown from March to July in drills lined with moist peat. The intermediates follow and are sown from late April to early June in rows 20 to 30 cm (8 to 12 in) apart. As the carrots start to grow they can be thinned a little during each visit to the garden, the thinnings used in casseroles or added to salads. Carrot fly is the main trouble and can be offset to some degree by dusting between the rows with soot or calomel dust, or watering with Jeyes Fluid (1 teaspoonful to 4·5 litres (1 gallon)) after thinning. It helps also to keep this pest away if the carrots are sown between rows of parsley (which germinates best if boiling water is poured down the seed drills before sowing) or garlic.

Swedes. A useful winter vegetable, they can play their part in crop rotation by following after or preceding brassicas. They may be sown at 10 cm (4 in) apart from mid-May to June, and the roots may either be left in the ground or lifted in mid-winter, then packed in boxes or black polythene bags with soil or moist peat and put in semi-darkness to yield tasty blanched shoots for use as spring greens. This method can also be followed with turnips.

Apples and Pears. Apples, ripening slowly as they do over several weeks, are a better proposition for the weekend gardener than such a pear as 'William's Bon Chrétien' which soon becomes over-soft. The firmer 'Conference', however, can be picked when opportune and stored until actually ready for eating, as also can 'Doyenne du Comice'. It is essential with most varieties to have a suitable pollinator. Compatible pears, apart from the self-fertile 'Conference', include 'Triomphe de Vienne' which can be gathered in August for September eating, 'Thompson's' to provide fruit for October and November, and 'Glou Morceau' which not only acts as an efficient pollinator for 'Doyenne du Comice' but provides sweet yellow pears for winter use.

If you intend planting your fruit trees in the rough grass areas which are such a help in enabling the weekend gardener to cope with an over-large garden, it is best to choose full standards which allow one to mow beneath the branches with ease. Standard apples should be grafted on M.XIV or M.XXV stocks and set 4·5 m (15 ft) apart each way. Usually, however, they take longer to start bearing than do the pyramid type.

Before planting, the soil should be broken up well in advance, taking care to keep the sub-soil to the bottom and digging in plenty of compost. It is best, however, not to incorporate farmyard manure just before planting unless the ground is very poor, and care should be taken to keep the bulge on the stems where the graft was made 5 cm (2 in) above the soil.

Apple varieties to give a long succession of blossom and fruit include the early 'Arthur Turner', one of the prettiest flowering trees which yields cooking apples to pick from July, thinning the crop so as to produce large 'bakers' in October and November; 'Laxton's Epicure'; 'Laxton's Early Crimson'; 'American Mother'; and 'Heusgen's Golden Reinette'—a succession that will give eating apples from mid-summer until the following April.

Other good varieties include 'Edward VII', a large cooking apple with good keeping qualities which often lasts until March, and 'Crawley Beauty', a dual-purpose apple that can be used from October to March either for eating or cooking. The delicious 'Cox's Orange Pippin' is also worth growing and should be placed near 'Arthur Turner' or 'Red Ellison' to ensure adequate pollination.

Apples and pears are beautiful in blossom as well as in fruit so it makes sense to grow complementary bulbs in the cleared ground beneath their branches. Grape hyacinths, daffodils and narcissi, and Spanish bluebells are all suitable and may be accompanied by primroses and violets. The finest wild garden we ever had was made in an apple orchard where the old-fashioned cottage paeonies flowered in cut circles, a variety of narcissi drifted through the grass, and primroses, grape hyacinths, dog violets, lungwort and forget-me-nots bloomed beneath the trees. Old-fashioned columbines, Queen Anne's Lace and meadow sweet kept a succession of beauty and interest until July when the grass was scythed.

In this chapter it has been possible only to lay down brief guide lines as to the most useful and easily grown crops for the absent gardener to try. Those who want to go deeper into the subject are recommended to read Joy Larkcom's *Vegetables For Small Gardens* (Faber), or the very useful RHS publications on the subject. There is also an excellent small book on *Fruit and Vegetables* edited by Peter Hunt, in the Pan Library of Gardening (Pan Books).

NINE

Cut Flowers and Pot Plants

Most gardeners enjoy flower arranging, and the weekender who owns a country or seaside garden has an advantage over many in being able to use it to grow as much decorative material as possible, greatly cutting down on the expense of bought flowers in town.

Even the smallest garden can be planned to provide for the house flowers, foliage, stems or seed-heads throughout the year without in any way detracting from its own pleasing effect. Fortunately, plants that are attractive for indoor use are equally effective in the garden, so that by planting with an eye to cutting one is actually improving the garden scene.

In sheer bounty of flower, the easier shrubs excel—most in a year or two being sufficiently large and free with their blooms to serve as a focal point for a particular area in the garden, and at the same time yielding blossom enough and to spare so that one can cut branches for the house and have the pleasure of building up a really important arrangement without robbing the garden scene. Luckily, such cutting if judiciously done can take the place of pruning, and it greatly softens the blow of having to leave the garden to return to town if one can take along branches of budding bloom from a shrub that one would otherwise miss seeing at its best.

Winter is the time when cut material is at the highest premium but even the coldest, bleakest garden can yield something pleasant, be it only the scarlet stems of *Cornus alba*, dogwood, or the purple of *Salix daphnoides*, violet willow, which later opens into prettily furred catkins. Milder gardens can add the jade of *Leycesteria formosa*, and the drooping, heavily ridged, sage-green leaves and velvet-encased flower and leaf buds of the tall-growing *Viburnum rhytidophyllum*. For foliage there is the evergrey *Senecio greyi* which is attractive in leaf throughout the year and bears clusters of sunny daisies in summer. *Elaeagnus pungens*

'Variegata' is one of the best foliage shrubs for winter with shiny dark-green leaves liberally splashed with gold.

For winter flowers, *Jasminum nudiflorum* is most reliable and its buds open indoors to the well-known, primrose stars. It can be grown either trained to a wall or making a mounded scrambler in the open. *Prunus subhirtella* 'Autumnalis', autumn cherry, opens its small white or pink flower sprays in mild spells throughout the winter, even in such bleak areas as the midland North Staffordshire where I grew up. Branches cut in bud and taken back to town will open their buds in succession over a long period, often eventually unfurling bright jade-green leaves when the flowers have dropped. Ribes, flowering currant, may be cut just before Christmas when its flowers will open to pure white and be totally innocent of the characteristic smell which some people find obnoxious. Forsythias, cut in January, will open within two or three weeks indoors, as will chaenomeles, Japanese quince, of which the varieties 'Aurora' and 'Phyllis Moore' are the earliest to bloom.

Given an acid soil, camellias might be added, of which the best all-rounder is *C.* × *williamsii* 'Donation' with luscious, double pink flowers. For a succession, we have found *C. japonica* 'Adolphe Audus-son', with perfectly shaped, semi-double scarlet blooms, to flower freely and well. Again for acid soil, the scented *Hamamelis mollis*, witch hazel, with golden maroon-centred, spider flowers, the paler *H. m.* 'Pallida' and the orange *H.* × *intermedia* 'Jelena' give over a month of bloom and last well when cut.

On acid soils they might be followed in earliest spring by the small rhododendron hybrid 'Praecox' with its rosy-mauve, azalea-type blooms. Later the host of dwarf species and the multitude of hybrids come into flower.

Yellow is not a colour one automatically associates with rhododen-drons but some of the yellows are among the most satisfactory to arrange. One of the prettiest is 'Diane', hardy and most accommodating with shapely leaves and trusses of large primrose flowers touched with scarlet at the throat. Slightly more tender and rather later is the biscuit-yellow 'Carita' and the deeper-coloured 'Hawk'. 'Lady Swaythling' (something sold as 'Gladys') is a soft lemon with shapely informal trusses. Scented rhododendrons, too, are exciting and 'Naomi' has a fresh cool scent and large heads of biscuit-and-soft-pink trumpets. Unusual and beautiful, too, is 'Lady Chamberlain' in its various colour forms based on salmon and yellow with narrow, trumpet flowers and small, oval-shaped, verdigris leaves. It might be followed in June by the long-blooming 'Fabia' with its informal trusses of terracotta flowers.

On lime and chalk, the glory of the rhododendrons has to be replaced by the chaenomeles; *Stachyurus praecox* with its ropes of yellow catkins; and viburnums such as the early blooming *V.* × *burkwoodii* which opens its sweetly scented, bun-shaped heads in a long succession from January to May, the later *V. juddii* and the summer-flowering *V. plicatum* 'Rowallane' which is a flower arranger's delight when its tiered branches are afoam with creamy lace-cap heads. The snowball-flowered *V. plicatum* itself is also good and *V. opulus*, the common guelder rose, is well worth planting, yielding as it does quantities of lace-caps followed by glistening red, translucent autumn fruits.

Apples are the ideal fruit for the weekender's garden and where there are established trees, the odd branch might well be spared, not only to lessen the future load, but to provide country-fresh blossom to take back to town. Of the purpose-grown, ornamental crab apples it is wise to choose such dual-purpose sorts as are mentioned in Chapter Five, which add to their showy flowers the bonus of long-lasting colourful fruits.

Most people enjoy the fragrance of philadelphus, mock orange, in the garden but often find it cloying indoors. One that is free of this charge is *P.* 'Belle Etoile' with its refreshing orange pekoe scent. It is also one of the best to arrange, with well-spaced squarish blooms stained at the centres with purple.

Late summer is a trying time both as regards garden colour and in respect of material to cut. Hydrangeas are a useful standby and their blooms last up to a fortnight if cut below the node and slit upwards through the joint for 8 cm (3 in) or more. In cold areas *H. paniculata* 'Grandiflora' can be grown, but in milder distances the magnificent 'Altona', 'Parsifal' and the dwarf 'Vulcan' are decorative over a very long period as their heads turn from raspberry pink or kingfisher blue to the purples, greens and crimsons of age. To last the winter they should be cut in mid-September as the heads begin to turn colour. The leaves should be removed and the stems stood in a very little water in a warm place such as a linen cupboard or boiler room to enable them to dry quickly. The quicker they dry, the better they keep their colour. Once dried they should be stored in a box or dry place until required.

In autumn, coloured leaves and berries are invaluable to support the dahlias, chrysanthemums and the exotic-looking nerines which can be quite easily grown in a well-drained, sunny house-border where the soil is not too poor. Thoughtfully placed, the berrying shrubs can provide an effective autumn backdrop to the garden display as well as yielding material of subtle beauty for arrangements indoors.

Snowberries, such as *Symphoricarpus* 'Constance Spry' and the pink
S. 'Magic Berry', will afford sprays of marble-size fruit to add distinc-
tion to groups of white or pink chrysanthemums. The large-leafed
Vitis coignetiae can decorate an arbour or pergola throughout the summer and in autumn its leaves will turn to orange, pink and purple,
making a sumptuous setting for arrangements of scarlet and apricot
dahlias, supplemented by sprays of blackberries or grapes.

Dahlias are sometimes difficult to keep through the winter. In some
areas they may be left in the garden, but if you are not sure whether
they will come through the winter outdoors you should lift them as
soon as the first frost has blackened the foliage. We always leave the
soil on the tubers, cut the stems down to 15 cm (6 in), label them as to
variety, height and colour, and bury them 13 cm (5 in) deep in a box of
dry peat. The box may be taken back with you after a weekend and
stored in a garage, attic or spare room until February, when it should
be watered occasionally until the shoots appear. It should then be
taken, if possible, on to the patio or a sunny balcony, stood against a
wall and covered with a sheet of glass. At night the box should be
covered with sacking until April when the worst frosts should be past.
Gradually the glass is left off by day and in May or June the dahlias can
be taken down to the country and planted in their flowering sites.

To the country, at the same time also, go the indoor plants to be sunk
to the rims of their pots in the soil in a semi-shaded spot. In this way,
azaleas, cyclamen, even the tender white jasmine or bougainvillea can
be kept to flower from year to year. We take our pots indoors again at
the beginning of September, and by watering them regularly bring
them on for another season of flower.

Pot plants left in town over the weekend or during a longer holiday
period need special care. The easiest way to cope for a period of up to a
week is to put each plant after watering into a clear polythene bag and,
trapping as much air as possible into the bag, make it airtight with a
rubber band, sticky tape or clip. The condensation forming inside the
bag will keep the plant moist.

Self-watering plant containers are also available and these will keep
the plants going for three to four weeks.

Another method which lasts for several weeks is to cut a wick into
15 cm (6 in) lengths, gently tap the plants out of their pots, remove any
drainage crocks and push one of the wicks up through the hole at the
bottom of each pot, splaying out the inserted end. Then replace the
plants. Using a bowl of water for each pot or the sink or bath containing about 10 cm (4 in) of water, stand the pots on inverted seed

trays, soap-dishes or something similar to keep the bases clear of the water, allowing the free ends of the wicks to be immersed for 5 to 8 cm (2 to 3 in).

Delightful pot plants to brighten the town house or flat in winter can be obtained simply by digging up clumps of primroses, violets, snowdrops or grape hyacinths from the weekend garden and potting them.

Bulbs set in pots or bowls in autumn can be wrapped in black polythene and left in the country until the shoots are well through, when they can be taken up to town. Small bulbs such as snowdrops, crocuses, dwarf irises, grape hyacinths and scillas, are best sunk, in bowls, into the soil of the country garden and left there until the buds show colour. If small bulbs of this sort are taken into the warmth too soon, they frequently go 'blind' and refuse to flower.

After the blooms have faded, daffodils, tulips, hyacinths and any small bulbs should be taken back to the country at the first opportunity and planted out into the garden where the leaves can wither and build up the bulbs to flower another season out-of-doors. Several years of recovery will usually be needed before the bulbs are ready again for indoor use; meanwhile they will be pleasant additions to the out-of-town garden and their blooms can always be cut for indoor use.

TEN

Pests and Diseases

In these days when the various chemical companies are spending vast sums on advertising to boost their products, the amateur gardener must be wary of becoming trigger-happy with chemicals. More harm has been done by the inadvertent swallowing of weedkillers and pesticides or undue contact with systemics—quite apart from long-term biological effects—than by the presence of holes in brassica leaves or the defoliation of roses due to black spot!

One should of course take sensible precautions to prevent the spread of pests and diseases in the garden, but where possible this should be accomplished by relatively harmless means. It is criminal to allow one's over-enthusiasm for a clinically clean garden to override the safety factor, especially when children, pets or birds may suffer.

The more powerful pesticides become, the more nervous I am of using them and the more I find myself returning to the well-tried and comparatively harmless remedies of my grandfather's time. Discover, for instance, the number of insect pests that can be dissuaded from attacking vegetables simply sprinkling a layer of soot along the drills before you sow the seed. True, soot may not be easily obtainable these days, but in that event try damping half a bucket of sand with paraffin and spreading a low ridge of it on either side of each seed row. This works, too, with the transplanted seedlings, discouraging both flying and crawling pests from their predations.

The main garden pests are slugs, snails, aphis—including greenfly, whitefly and blackfly which suck the sap from leaves and stem, often transmitting diseases in the process—caterpillars, some beetles, carrot and onion flies, chafer bugs, leatherjackets, wireworms, cutworms, millipedes, mice and pigeons.

Nothing can stop cabbage-white butterflies from coming down and alighting on the leaves of cabbage plants. Luckily, however, it is not the butterflies themselves that do the damage; it is the caterpillars which hatch from the eggs they lay on the leaf surfaces. These egg deposits are easily spotted, so if you can go round your cabbage rows daily after sunset, you can rub off the eggs between your finger and thumb.

Where absence from the garden has allowed an infestation of caterpillars to overtake you, dose each cabbage with a syringing of salted water—a small handful of salt to a 9 litre (2 gal) bucket of water. The spraying should always be done after sunset.

Insecticides of some sort must be used in both the flower and the vegetable gardens, so it is important to select those which have the least harmful effects on human, domestic animal or bird life. In our own garden, we use liquid derris supplemented by a pyrethrum puffer. Liquid derris will give protection from aphis, and may be used on roses. Pyrethrum dust controls aphis, caterpillars and flea beetle. Derris dust is also effective against the latter two pests. Derived as they are from plants, both derris and pyrethrum may be considered safer than many synthetic chemicals; mixed together they give even greater control over pests.

Against slugs and snails, crushed potassium permanganate crystals mixed with fine sand is an effective remedy; scatter the crystals on the ground from a tin with a sprinkler lid.

Jeyes Fluid is a good deterrent against carrot fly and other soil pests and will also help to prevent club root in brassicas.

Mice can be thwarted by surrounding plantings of vulnerable bulbs with the prickly shoots of holly or gorse. Similarly such shoots may be placed along the pea rows. Alternatively, crocuses and other small bulbs may be planted in 'parcels' of fine-mesh wire. Wire pea guards, used to protect the rows from bird predators, will also protect against mice if sunk into the ground for 5 cm (2 in) on either side of the row. Mice and moles are often the cause of failure with lily bulbs and here again wire mesh is the answer, a cylinder of mesh being sunk into the ground to surround each bulb 'station'.

A friend of ours sets his precious *Lilium auratum* seedlings in drainpipes sunk into the soil and filled with appropriately rich acid compost. He has found this method to be completely successful.

Birds can be kept away from primroses, polyanthus, seedlings and crops by the use of criss-crossed lines of cotton, milk-bottle tops strung tautly over the rows, toy windmills struck into the ground, or red-painted jam jars placed upside down on sticks. Soft fruit, however, must be netted to keep the marauders out, and for those who like myself hate to see young birds entrapped in strawberry netting the only answer is to erect a complete wire cage in which the fruit can ripen unharmed.

Although birds can be a nuisance, it should be remembered that much good is done by the many small birds which devour insects and other pests.

Should you decide to use any of the more powerful chemicals in your garden, do treat them with respect, following the maker's instructions carefully and wearing protective gloves and possibly goggles and mask. Spraying should be carried out on windless days and preferably during the evening. Watering cans which have contained weedkillers or other deadly chemicals should never be washed or filled at the kitchen sink or domestic washbasin. Try always to use an outside tap and remember to wash both the equipment and your own hands carefully afterwards. Should any of the chemicals come in contact with your skin, be sure to wash them off immediately. Most important, keep all chemicals and spray equipment out of the reach of children and pets. Weedkillers and systemics should always be treated as potentially dangerous and religiously locked away.

As an alternative to using chemicals, there are various organic methods which are worth a trial.

Aphis. These may be deterred by a sowing of nasturtiums below fruit trees. Summer pruning, too, serves the same end—by removing the soft wood which is subject to attack. Moreover, except for tip-bearing apple trees such as 'Worcester Pearmain', this cutting back of long growth in July to two or three buds will build up a spur system leading to better quality and more prolific crops.

Carrot fly. This may be controlled by sowing a catch crop of spring onions between the rows; the insects apparently dislike the smell of onions. A thick mulch—1·5 cm (½ in)—of lawn mowings between the rows will also blanket the smell that attracts the insects. Alternatively, one can sow pelleted seed to avoid the need to thin out the seedlings which disturbs the soil, and releases the scent to the fly.

It is appropriate to mention here another method of deterring this pest. After thinning, immediately dampen the soil along the rows and then knead down firmly with the fist. At the same time make doubly sure by mixing about half a litre (1 pint) of paraffin into the 9 litre (2 gal) bucketful of water you are using for the purpose. To get the paraffin and water to mix, first beat into the paraffin an equal quantity of milk and then add the mixture to the water. Our grandparents used this method and it always seemed to work.

Ants. These must be dealt with mercilessly and the safest way is to mix 57 ml (2 fl oz) each of pyrethum and derris with 9 l (2 gal) of water

and pour this solution into the nest by way of a piece of hosepipe.
Apple-blossom weevil. This pest may be defeated by binding strips
of sacking 15 cm (6 in) wide round the trunks (just beneath the branches)
in June, to be removed in October with their load of pests.
Capsid bugs. They will succumb to a similar method but in their case
the bands should be positioned in early spring. Newspapers edged with
sticky banding may be used similarly to catch the green capsid bugs
which attack gooseberries, currants, roses and flowering shrubs.
Big bud. This is caused by a tiny mite that works its way into the buds
of the new shoots in June to lay its eggs. It is the feeding and breeding
of the young mites that cause the abnormal swelling of the buds and
the resultant 'blindness'. As a control, all enlarged buds should be
picked off in July, November and again in early March, and burned.
Between mid-March and mid-April the bushes should be sprayed with
a pyrethum and derris mixture.
Blackfly. One can usually avoid this by sowing one's broad beans in
autumn and picking out the tips before the aphis have a chance to
swarm. Sowings of 'Windsor' varieties in early June to crop in August
also miss the pests.

Another useful tip (for which I am indebted to Messrs Thompson
and Morgan) is to sow summer savoury among the broad beans. The
savoury keeps the aphis at bay and can be harvested and cooked with
the beans to give a superb flavour. This method is practised by Dutch
growers.

True diseases are caused by fungi, bacteria and viruses, against which
appropriate precautions can usually be taken. Other so-called diseases
are really ailments due to malfunctioning of the plants caused by outside factors—lack of water, mineral deficiency, soil imbalance due to
over-liming or too much artificial fertilizer. Many of these need never
occur. Often diseases can be offset by simple mechanical precautions.
Brassica club root. This is rife if these vegetables are grown in over-
acid soils. The commonsense remedy is to determine just how much
lime your soil needs by purchasing a simple soil-test kit from your
chemist or garden shop, carrying out the tests as directed and adminis-
tering lime at the rate suggested. Lime is a slow-acting treatment and
will not be effective until twelve to eighteen months after application.
Meanwhile peas and beans should be grown and the soil green-
manured or allowed to lie fallow during the winter. Potatoes should not
be grown until after the next brassica crop, as they are prone to scab if
grown in limy soil. The practice of crop rotation is also a vital factor.
Brassica and allied plants must never be grown on the same ground

E

two seasons in succession. A good system of rotation is to divide the ground up into three. Plot A will grow the brassica family during the first year while Plot B is devoted to peas, beans, celery and leeks and Plot C grows potatoes and other root vegetables.

In the second year the subjects planted on Plot A during the first year are transferred to Plot B, while those on Plot B are grown on Plot C and those on Plot C move over to Plot A. The third year sees another change-round—each subject moving on again in similar fashion so that it is not until the fourth year that brassicas are again grown on Plot A.

Additionally, one can smash up the old-fashioned naptha moth balls, putting a fragment in each hole at planting time as a remedy against club root.

Potato blight. This can best be avoided by growing early varieties which will reach full weight and keep like the maincrop kinds. 'Duke of York' is an old variety which is still worth growing for this purpose. Before the dark brown patches indicative of blight appear on the leaves they will have almost finished their growth and little will be lost by cutting the haulm off at ground level and composting it before it has time to blacken. You should then wait a fortnight before lifting the potatoes so that the spores lying on the surface of the ground are no longer virulent and liable to infect the crop as it is dug.

Peach leaf curl. This unsightly blight affects ornamental almonds, peaches and apricots as well as those grown for fruit. The answer to this nuisance is to spray while the trees are leafless and before the buds begin to swell, with 90 g (3 oz) of copper sulphate that has been mixed overnight with 4½ l (1 gal) of hot water and to which has been added, when cool, a solution of 120 g (4 oz) of washing soda in 4½ l (1 gal) of cold water.

Apple and Pear scab. These may also be dealt with by the same mixture applied in February or early March, before the leaves appear. Unlike the more usual lime-sulphur mixture it does not destroy the useful *Anthocoris nemorum* which preys on red spider, nor upset the sulphur-sensitive 'James Grieve', 'Cox's Orange', 'Beauty of Bath' and 'Worcester Pearmain' apples, nor the 'William' and 'Louis Ronne of Jersey' pears. The delicious 'Doyenne du Comice' is susceptible to both lime-sulphur and copper so the only remedy here is the now difficult to obtain Burgundy Mixture.

Black spot. This disease gives rose enthusiasts much heartache, but a great deal can be done to prevent it if all affected foliage is picked off and burned when the symptoms are first noticed. At the end of the season any withered stems or dead wood, together with any fallen leaves, must be incinerated. The disease spores fall to the ground and over-winter there, so during the late winter a mulch of peat should be applied and a solution of Jeyes Fluid (1 teaspoon to 4½ l (1 gal) of water, or as directed on the tin) liberally applied over the peat. Routine spraying as soon as the leaves open the following season and repeated whenever possible should then help to keep the plants healthy.

For a time it seemed that Maneb was the answer to the trouble, then that Benlate was to end black spot for all time. Both are undoubtedly good but many large growers now find it necessary to continually change the spray as the fungi become resistant to the different remedies. For my part, I think that most roses will be kept in good health if the proper precautions are followed and the roses sprayed or dusted with Captan for black spot and Karathene for mildew, mulching with grass clippings being kept up throughout the summer or the ground beneath the roses being covered with the foliage of carpeting plants such as violas.

Appendixes
including
Garden Designs
drawn by
YVONNE SCARGON

Garden Designs

1 and 2. These two plans show a cottage garden as purchased and the same garden after it has been replanned and rationalized for ease of maintenance on a weekend gardener basis. The front garden which was a 'cottage' jumble of perennial plants, dahlias and chrysanthemums has been put down to rough grass to reduce maintenance. In this area is planted a variety of apple trees—cookers and eaters—to provide fruit to enjoy at the weekend, to take back to town and to store for winter when the cost of fruit is high. Bulbs planted in the grass provide for spring colour.

A small vegetable garden has been kept at the side to provide salads, runner beans, and such vegetables as New Zealand spinach, onions and broccoli which require little care if mulched against drought and weeds.

A terrace has been provided at the rear for outdoor living. This is flanked by floribunda roses for cutting, underplanted by the white and purple forms of *Viola cornuta* which will interbreed to provide a mixture of colours: as long as the dead heads are removed at weekends, both the roses and the violas will give flower from May until late October. Under the south-facing windows, the bright yellow flowers of the winter jasmine, *Jasminum nudiflorum*, are welcome in late winter and an ornamental quince, either *Chaenomeles speciosa* (popularly known as Japonica) or *C.* × *superba*, provides colour in varying shades of red in early spring, followed later on by attractive yellow or greenish-yellow fruits. There is a pergola at the far end of the garden, covered with a vine to provide a shady place to sit in hot weather, and herbs and lavenders have been introduced. An island bed of small shrubs and perennials in the lawn is largely self-maintaining and can be planted to give colour and interest in all seasons. By mingling the winter-blooming hellebores and early spring-flowering periwinkles with doronicum, nepeta, perovskia and such shrubs as the dwarf philadelphus, 'Manteau d' Hermine', *Syringa pallabiniana*, potentilla and caryopteris, the bed can be kept bright for much of the year.

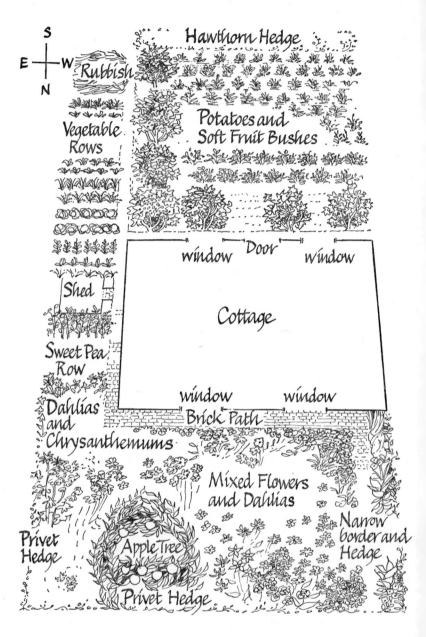

S
E ✛ W
N

Hawthorn Hedge

Rubbish

Potatoes and
Soft Fruit Bushes

Vegetable
Rows

window   Door   window

Shed

Cottage

Sweet Pea
Row

window   window

Dahlias
and
Chrysanthemums

Brick Path

Mixed Flowers
and Dahlias

Privet
Hedge

Narrow
border and
Hedge

Apple Tree

Privet Hedge

I   COTTAGE GARDEN AS PURCHASED
14 M X 40 M   (45 FT X 130 FT)

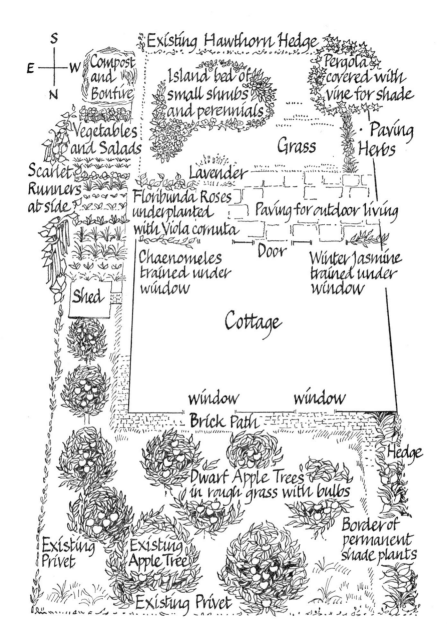

S
E — **W**
N

Compost and Bonfire

Existing Hawthorn Hedge

Island bed of small shrubs and perennials

Pergola covered with vine for shade

Paving Herbs

Vegetables and Salads

Grass

Scarlet Runners at side

Lavender

Floribunda Roses underplanted with Viola cornuta

Paving for outdoor living

Shed

Chaenomeles trained under window

Door

Winter Jasmine trained under window

Cottage

window   window

Brick Path

Hedge

Dwarf Apple Trees in rough grass with bulbs

Existing Privet

Existing Apple Tree

Border of permanent shade plants

Existing Privet

SAME GARDEN RATIONALIZED FOR WEEKEND USE
14 M X 40 M (45 FT X 130 FT)

3. A fairly large garden of a weekend cottage designed for easy maintenance and for survival during the owner's fairly long periods of absence. A sizeable area of paving to the side and front gives opportunity for outdoor living and reduces the area near to the cottage which needs to be kept neat.

A commune of summer-blooming, sun-loving plants in the irregularly-shaped island bed is largely self-maintaining and able to resist drought. At the edge of the paving, a bed for bulbs with ground cover would provide for spring and autumn interest. Winter, too, could be colourful if the planting were to include *Cyclamen oribculatum, Galanthus elwesii* and the very early, bright blue *Iris histroides major,* Underplanted with dwarf ivies such as *Hedera helix* 'Gold Heart' and 'Glacier', the bulbs would spear through the foliage with ease while the ivy leaves would serve the two-fold purpose of decoration and protection. Muscari, species tulips and small daffodil hybrids for later spring might be followed in autumn by South African schizostylis and the glamorous nerines.

The large area of lawn need be cut only with a rotary mower when the cottage is occupied, the surrounding high grass being planted with the larger daffodils and narcissi and cut only when the foliage has withered and again in August so that the easily-naturalized *Crocus speciosus* and the colchicums can make their autumn show.

Apple trees have been chosen for beauty of blossom and usefulness of fruit while the glowing 'crabs' of *Malus* 'Golden Hornet' can be either left to decorate the garden or used for jelly. *Prunus subhirtella* 'Autumnalis' is one of the most satisfactory and longest-lasting trees for winter display and the foliage of the silver-leafed weeping pear, *Pyrus salicifolia* 'Pendula' is restfully graceful from spring to frost.

Chaenomeles, forsythia, weigela and the shrub roses might be chosen for the self-care border to mingle with such easy perennials as astilbes, astrantia, *Chrysanthemum maximum* 'Esther Read', the hardy *Agapanthus* Headbourne Hybrids, *Salvia superba*, the grey-leafed *Stachys lanata*, and the long-flowering, cherry-pink potentilla 'Miss Wilmott'.

The rose 'Golden Showers' on the south-facing trellis has a long-flowering season and looks well with the rich blue of the neighbouring evergreen *Ceanothus* 'Burkwoodii'.

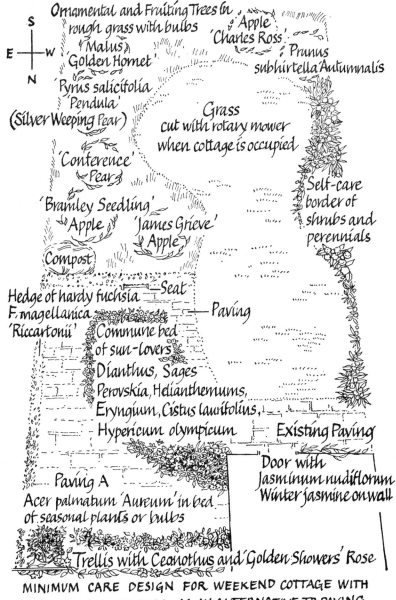

S E W N

Ornamental and Fruiting Trees in rough grass with bulbs

'Malus Golden Hornet'

Apple 'Charles Ross'

Prunus subhirtella 'Autumnalis'

Pyrus salicifolia 'Pendula' (Silver Weeping Pear)

Grass cut with rotary mower when cottage is occupied

'Conference' Pear

Self-care border of shrubs and perennials

'Bramley Seedling' Apple

'James Grieve' Apple

Compost

Hedge of hardy fuchsia F. magellanica 'Riccartonii'

Seat

Paving

Commune bed of sun-lovers Dianthus, Sages Perovskia, Helianthemums, Eryngium, Cistus laurifolius, Hypericum olympicum

Existing Paving

Door with Jasminum nudiflorum Winter jasmine on wall

Paving A Acer palmatum 'Aureum' in bed of seasonal plants or bulbs

Trellis with Ceanothus and 'Golden Showers' Rose

MINIMUM CARE DESIGN FOR WEEKEND COTTAGE WITH LARGE GARDEN AT REAR. AS AN ALTERNATIVE TO PAVING, THE SPACE MARKED 'A' COULD BE USED FOR VEGETABLES IF PREFERRED

3

14 M X 34 M (45 FT X 110 FT)

4. The garden of a large weekend cottage, resulting from a two cottage conversion. The dividing hedge between the gardens was removed and the gardens treated as one entity when viewed from the windows of the large sitting room opening on to the paved terrace.

One difficulty was that the garden faced north. This meant that the paved area near the house was more a convention of design than a practical place for sitting out. With a silver-leafed weeping pear (*Betula* 'Youngii' the weeping silver birch, would be an acceptable alternative) planted in the paving at one side and *Camellia* 'Donation', the finest of the × *williamsii* hybrids, against a wall, this area is pleasant and requires virtually no maintenance. Added interest might be obtained by the planting of winter-blooming heaths, followed by campanulas for summer, in sites in the paving.

The garden pictured is in a mild area. In colder districts, the camellia on the east wall might be more satisfactorily replaced by the tasselled wall shrub, *Garrya elliptica*. The camellia blooms might otherwise be spoiled by morning sun following frost at night.

Opposite the patio doors of the sitting-room a straight path leads from the terrace to a lawn and sitting-out area facing south. The path is flanked by floribunda roses underplanted with *Viola cornuta*. Alternatively the pink *Geranium endressii* mingled with *G.* × *wallichianum* 'Buxton's Blue' might be used. Beyond the borders on either side three dwarf apple trees are planted in rough grass.

Flanking the lawn is an informal pebble bed covered with a mixture of small shrubs and perennials underplanted with ground cover, mulched until the subjects touched. (As the soil is acid, an alternative would be to plant evergreen azaleas and some heaths, together with *Acer palmatum* 'Dissectum'.)

Hostas and day lilies are grown at the other side of the lawn against a panelled fence. A vegetable plot has been provided far to the left of the garden beyond an easy-care bed of hardy shrubs underplanted with vincas, epimediums and hellebores.

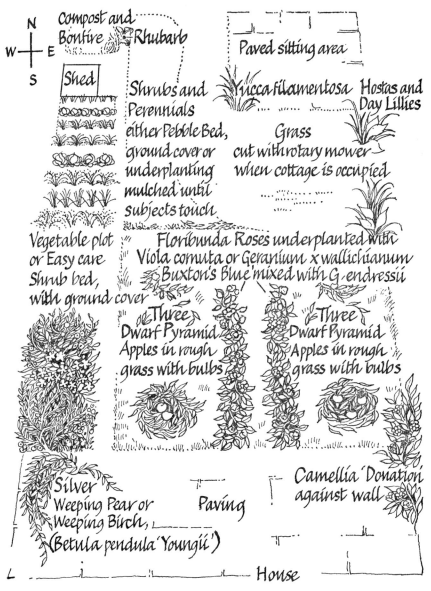

N
W — E
S

Compost and
Bonfire · Rhubarb

Paved sitting area

Shed

Shrubs and
Perennials
either Pebble Bed,
ground cover or
underplanting
mulched until
subjects touch

Yucca filamentosa

Hostas and
Day Lillies

Grass
cut with rotary mower
when cottage is occupied

Vegetable plot
or Easy care
Shrub bed,
with ground cover

Floribunda Roses underplanted with
Viola cornuta or Geranium x wallichianum
'Buxton's blue' mixed with G. endressii

Three
Dwarf Pyramid
Apples in rough
grass with bulbs

Three
Dwarf Pyramid
Apples in rough
grass with bulbs

Silver
Weeping Pear or
Weeping Birch,
(Betula pendula 'Youngii')

Paving

Camellia 'Donation'
against wall

House

EASY-CARE GARDEN FOR LARGE WEEKEND COTTAGE
RESULTING FROM TWO COTTAGE CONVERSION
24M X 43M (80FT X 140FT)

4

5. The garden of a typical terraced cottage conversion. In the small front garden the privet hedge has been left against the path leading to the door, but removed from the front and side where it would be too greedy, replaced at the front by the clippable, slow-growing *Berberis darwinii* with showy orange flowers in spring and neat small holly-like leaves. The dividing boundary has been marked by panelling 1·5 m (5 ft) high on which are trained a late-fruiting pyracantha, the berries of which are usually spared by the birds, and *Clematis* 'Nelly Moser' which will succeed in a north-east exposure. *Jasminum nudiflorum* is trained beneath the sitting-room window for winter bloom and the tiny garden is planted closely with dwarf rhododendrons and evergreen azaleas, along with chaenomeles, euphorbia and hellebores. On lime or chalk the rhododendrons could be replaced by daphnes and by skimmia, dwarf evergreen berberis or, in a mild area by *Fabiana* 'Prostrata' with its bluish-mauve flowers which appear in May and June and *Ceanothus prostratus* to form a carpet of bright blue in spring.

At the rear the brick paved area outside the back door is extended by broken paving set in cement in which spaces have been left for thyme, chamomile and other fragrant plants which do not suffer from being trodden underfoot. This gives a contrast in textures and at the same time extends the sitting area out of doors. At the side of the useful, already-existing path, herbs and salads are given space, together with sweet-scented bedding plants such as wallflowers and stocks, easily grown from seed or bought in for a reasonably modest sum as the area to be covered is small. Blackcurrants, gooseberries and rhubarb yield fruit for weekend pies or to make jam and are set around the existing 'Grenadier' apple which yields good quality fruit for cooking. Three climbing roses against the screen block wall that has replaced the old rather straggling privet give plentiful blooms for cutting in yellow ('Golden Showers'), scarlet ('Danse du Feu') and apricot-pink ('School-girl'). In the small lawn are set bushes of the extremely decorative *Viburnum plicatum* 'Rowallane' for May, with the white-flowered *Hydrangea* 'Mme Mouillière', *Potentilla* 'Tangerine' and the golden *Hypericum* 'Hidcote', along with a smoke tree, purple-leaved *Cotinus coggygria* 'Royal Purple', for contrast. Much of the small grass area is left rough and planted with bulbs, being cut with a Turk scythe or small Black and Decker rotor-mower when the bulb foliage has withered.

The informally shaped bed between the grass and the path is planted with such small shrubs as *Hydrangea* 'Vulcan', *Potentilla* 'Sunset', *Caryopteris clandonensis* and *Berberis thunbergii atropurpurea*, underplanted with hardy geraniums; decorative and cactus dahlias might also be interspersed.

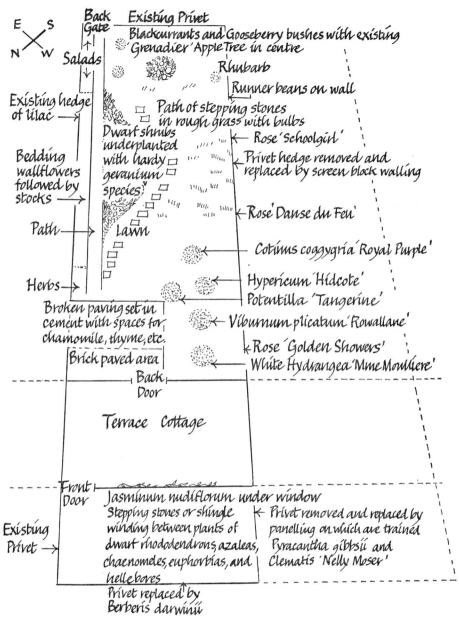

E S
N W

Back Gate

Existing Privet

Blackcurrants and Gooseberry bushes with existing 'Grenadier' Apple Tree in centre

Salads

Rhubarb

Runner beans on wall

Existing hedge of lilac →

Path of stepping stones in rough grass with bulbs

Dwarf shrubs underplanted with hardy geranium species

← Rose 'Schoolgirl'

Bedding wallflowers followed by stocks →

Privet hedge removed and replaced by screen block walling

← Rose 'Danse du Feu'

Path →

Lawn

Cotinus coggygria 'Royal Purple'

Herbs →

Hypericum 'Hidcote'

Potentilla 'Tangerine'

Broken paving set in cement with spaces for chamomile, thyme, etc.

← Viburnum plicatum 'Rowallane'

Brick paved area

← Rose 'Golden Showers'

White Hydrangea 'Mme Moulliere'

Back Door

Terrace Cottage

Front Door

Existing Privet →

Jasminum nudiflorum under window
Stepping stones or shingle winding between plants of dwarf rhododendrons, azaleas, chaenomeles, euphorbias, and hellebores

← Privet removed and replaced by panelling on which are trained Pyracantha gibbsii and Clematis 'Nelly Moser'

Privet replaced by Berberis darwinii

FRONT AND REAR GARDEN OF A TYPICAL VILLAGE TERRACED COTTAGE
4·5M X 30M (15FT X 100FT)

5

6. The garden of a modern bungalow, formerly permanently occupied, has been converted to make it suitable for weekend maintenance and enjoyment. Seasonal bedding round the front lawn has been replaced by heaths and heathers, thus considerably reducing the work of edging and weeding. The making of an irregularly shaped large island bed of heathers adds emphasis to the existing fine specimen of *Acer palmatum*; *Juniperus sabina tamariscifolia* is added for further interest, for being dwarf and spreading it contrasts usefully with the acer and also with the heathers. Year-round colour at the front of the house can be achieved by planting heathers such as *Calluna vulgaris* 'Golden Haze' and from the heaths one can select the *Erica carnea* varieties, among them the golden-foliaged 'Foxhollow', along with those of *E. cinerea* and *E. vagans*. For neatness and easy maintenance, it is suggested that the grass be replaced, if possible, by paving. A stark concrete-brick wall to the right of the gates is now disguised by *Cotoneaster horizontalis* and chaeonomeles and winter jasmine are trained against the panelling on both sides. Honeysuckle is grown at the side of the gate leading to the utility area occupied by compost and dustbins whilst camellia and hydrangea, underplanted with hellebores, in front of the panelling by the garden gate nearest the front door, have been chosen to give the longest possible season of interest.

At the rear, a side path has been eliminated and the broken paving used to extend the existing slab-paved small patio and provide a barbecue area: formerly fruit and vegetables were grown within sight of the original patio and also, through glass-panelled doors, of the sitting-room. A focal point is provided by a lead figure (or perhaps a bird bath), backed by a curve of potentillas fronting two contrasting *Juniperus media* cultivars in gold and green. This planting is effectively flanked by the small-growing weeping willow, *Salix purpurea* 'Pendula', trained as a standard, on one side and a weeping pear, *Pyrus salicifolia pendula*, on the other. Easy-care musk hybrid roses are set amongst fence-trained plants underplanted with long-lasting perennials.

Work is lessened by restricting the previous formal lawn to the area immediately in front of the patio and stepping stones, set in a mown path, then wind through rough grass which is roto-cut when the bulb foliage dies down.

An island bed of mixed hybrid tea roses has been replanted with shrubs and herbaceous ground cover. A selection of shrubs and trees, including some fruit trees, is set in the grass. Provision has been made for soft fruit, salad, vegetables and herbs, the latter conveniently grown by the back door.

Use is made of all available wall and fence space, both to soften the harshness of the larch-lap surround and to look interesting and attractive over a long period of time.

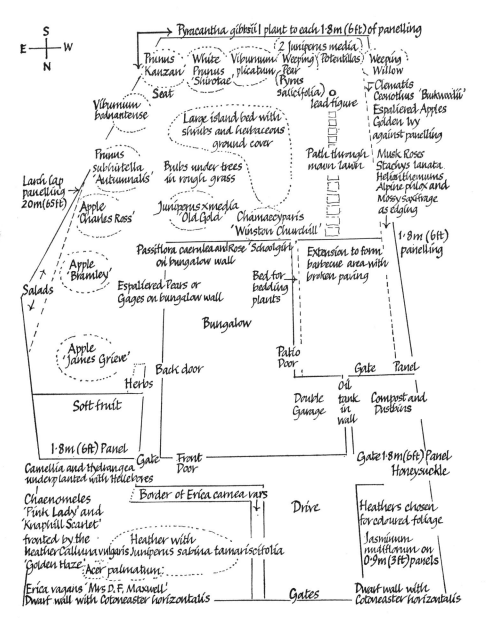

BUNGALOW WITH LARGE, IRREGULAR-SHAPED GARDEN
AFTER CONVERSION FOR EASY MAINTENANCE
ABOUT 0·15 HECTARES (⅓ ACRE)

Grass and Paving

Grass presents a problem unless the garden is to be visited each week-end. For this reason it is usually best to pave the front garden and the area of the back garden closest to the house. Alternatively the front garden may be turned into a picturesque little orchard with dwarf pyramid apples in rough grass planted with bulbs, columbines, fox-gloves, primroses, violets, etc.

If the back garden is large, much of the area can be treated the same way and here, if there is room, standard apples should be chosen to allow the mower to pass beneath. Where bulbs are grown, it must be remembered that the grass should not be cut until their foliage has died down; so that too much of the grass is not left shaggy for too long, it is wisest to restrict the planting area to the immediate surrounds of the trees. The remainder may be cut with a Flymo or similar rotary cutter whenever the garden is visited. If one has a good deal of land, it may be sufficient just to cut paths through the grass with the mower, leaving the rest to be scythed in June and October.

To have the garden professionally paved is expensive, but it should not be beyond the scope of many weekenders to do the job themselves, section by section, first cleaning the ground and levelling, then putting down an 8 cm (3 in) layer of ash, cinders or broken stone to form a drainage stratum as well as to provide a firm bed for the paving. Each stone should then be bedded in cement, also filling up the joints between the stones. Here and there, if one wishes, pockets may be left between the stones for dwarf thymes, campanulas, alpine phlox and similar plants which help drainage by absorbing surface water, as well as adding a great deal to the charm of a paved area.

If the ground is soft, the earth must be rammed hard before attempting to pave. It may also pay to lay down a 5 cm (2 in) bed of concrete before laying the stones.

A much simpler paving method consists of laying random paving on top of heavy black polythene spread over well-weeded earth, brushing a dry mortar of cement and sand (2 parts dry sand to 1 of cement) thickly over the paving and allowing the rain to wash it in. This, of course, has to be undertaken during the autumn or winter in order to be sure of sufficient rain.

This method can be improved on by spreading builder's, or sea, sand over the area to be paved and tamping it down well with a board to ensure a flat, firm surface before putting down the polythene. Where polythene is used drainage can sometimes be a problem so the area to be paved should always be canted slightly towards a grid or ditch.

A great advantage of this method is that the work can be done gradually over numerous weekends, paving in sections as time allows and as local stone or slate comes to hand. With an edging of tougher alpines spilling over to soften the paving, a most attractive result can be achieved.

Many country cottages have old brick paths which, although attractive, can be dangerously slippery in wet weather. They should be treated with Murphy's Super Moss Killer (obtainable from ironmongers and garden supply shops). Fifty-seven millilitres (2 fl oz) dissolved in 9 l (2 gal) water is enough to treat 8 sq m (9½ sq yd). The treatment should be repeated whenever the moss starts to reappear.

Compost

Home-made compost for use as a fertilizer, dug into the ground before planting or laid on top of the soil as a mulch, is an essential part of the economy of the garden.

Badly made compost can be a nuisance, spreading weed-seeds where they are not wanted, so it is worth taking the trouble to make a scientific heap. Today various purpose-made compost bins are available. In inconspicuous green plastic, they are not unsightly, and they make the job of composting easier.

Alternatively, you can build your own bin, setting two parallel posts at each corner, into which planks can be slipped or removed as required. The bottom planks at either end should rest on a pair of bricks to allow the air to pass beneath. The side planks then rest on the end planks. The next pair of end planks should rest on the side planks, and so on as necessary.

The base of the heap should rest upon the earth which should be forked over to improve drainage and facilitate the movement of earthworms into the heap. A coarse layer of tree prunings should go first into the bin to help aeration by lifting the base a little off the ground. After that comes household waste, in the form of vegetable prunings, egg shells, fruit skins, tea leaves or bags, vacuum cleaner fluff and old wool; garden waste such as annual weeds, pea haulms, chopped cabbage stalks, lawn mowings, bonfire ash; and any gathered material such as seaweed, green bracken and straw. These may be mixed with animal or fowl manure, concentrated manure, commercial activator or simply ammonium sulphate.

Perennial weeds or any woody or diseased material should never be used, nor should man-made materials such as Terylene, Crimplene, nylon fabrics or plastic, as these will not rot down. If the compost is destined primarily for the vegetable garden, lime may be added to the heap if your garden soil is acid, but lime and manure, or lime and activator, should never be added to the same layer. Instead, cover each layer with a thin spreading of soil and add a sprinkling of lime on top.

The compost heap should always be kept damp but not too wet. In some areas and during the winter it may be necessary to protect it from excessive rain with a cover. Some of the patent bins are already supplied with covers.

After about three weeks the heap should be turned sides to middle to give the outer edges a chance to rot. If this is not practicable, take off the outer edges and use them to start a second heap. Ideally two heaps should always be on the go—one in the process of rotting down and the other being built. Once a heap is completed it should be topped with an 8 cm (3 in) layer of soil and covered with sacks or black polythene sheeting. In summer, such a heap in four months will produce crumbly, black, rich compost ready for use. In winter it will take six months or more.

Many people who can get straw like to compost it. Straw can either be incorporated into the ordinary compost heap or built into a heap of its own. It should be laid in 15 cm (6 in) layers, each layer being watered until it is thoroughly moist. The alternate layers should be sprinkled in turn with lime or sulphate of ammonia, viz: straw—lime— straw—sulphate of ammonia. A straw heap can be stacked 1·2 to 2·5 m (4 to 5 ft) high and should be ready for use in under six months.

Some Recommended Suppliers

Bagged manure   Organic Concentrates Ltd, Loudhams Wood Lane, Chalfont St Giles, Bucks.

Compost bins   Compo-Quick, Deerhurst, Walton, Glos. Rotocrop Ltd, 848 Brighton Road, Purley, Surrey.

Plant supports   Scottish War Blinded, Room B, Linburn, Wilkiston, by Kirknewton, Midlothian.

Pulverized bark for mulching   A list of suppliers can be obtained from: Bark Products (Bristol) Ltd, Nethan Road, Bristol BS5 9PQ.

Soil-testing kit   Boots the Chemist and other stores dealing in horticultural goods.
Sudbury Technical Products Ltd, 58 Charlton Road, London SE3 8TT.

Bulbs–*choice small bulbs*   Broadleigh Gardens, Barr House, Bishop's Hull, Taunton, Somerset TA4 AE1.
–*other bulbs*   Walter Blom Ltd, Leavesden, Watford, Herts WD2 7BH.

Clematis   Fisks Nursery, Welteston, Saxmundham, Suffolk.
Pennell & Sons Ltd, 312 High Street, Lincoln.
Treasures Ltd, Tenbury Wells, Worcs.

Hardy heaths   Maxwell & Beale Ltd, Corfe Mullen, Wimborne, Dorset.

Hardy plants   Bressingham Hall Ltd, Diss, Norfolk.
Unusual Plants, White Barn House, Elmstead Market, Essex.

Rhododendrons and azaleas   Hillier & Sons Ltd, Winchester, Hants.
Bodnant Gardens, Tal-y-Cafn, Clwyd, N. Wales.

Roses   David Austin Ltd, Albrighton, Wolverhampton.

Seeds   Thompson & Morgan Ltd, London Road, Ipswich, Suffolk.

Shade plants   Newlake Gardens, Copthorne, Crawley, Surrey.

Shrubs   Hillier & Sons (as above).
Bodnant Gardens (as above).
Southdown Nurseries, Redruth, Cornwall.

Index

To avoid an over-long index, cultivar names have not been included.